KATE O'BRIEN

(1897–1974) was born in Limerick, Ireland, the fourth daughter of Catherine Thornhill and Thomas O'Brien. Her mother died when she was five and she was educated at Laurel Hill Convent, Limerick, and at University College, Dublin. Kate O'Brien lived in London for some years where she made her living as a journalist and began to write stories and plays. She also worked in Manchester, on the *Guardian*, and spent a year as a governess in Spain: a country she was to return to and write about often.

Kate O'Brien originally became known as a playwright, her first plays being *Distinguished Villa* (1926) and *The Bridge* (1927). But it was with the publication of her first novel, *Without My Cloak* (1931), that her work became widely acclaimed. Described by J. B. Priestly as a "particularly beautiful and arresting piece of fiction", it won the Hawthornden and the James Tait Black Prizes of 1931. This was followed by eight more novels: *The Ante-Room* (1934), *Mary Lavelle* (1936), *Pray for the Wanderer* (1938), *The Land of Spices* (1941), *The Last of Summer* (1943), *That Lady* (1946), *The Flower of May* (1953) and *As Music and Splendour* (1958). Two of these novels, *Mary Lavelle* and *The Land of Spices*, were censored for their "immorality" by the Irish Censorship Board. Kate O'Brien dramatised three of her novels, *That Lady* also being made into a film starring Olivia De Havilland; she wrote travel books: *Farewell Spain* (1937), and *My Ireland* (1962); an autobiography, *Presentation Parlour* (1963); English Diaries and Journals (1943); and a monograph on Teresa of Avila (1951). Her works have been translated into French, German, Spanish, Czech and Swedish.

After a brief marriage at the age of twenty-six Kate O'Brien remained single for the rest of her life. In 1947 she was elected a member of the Irish Academy of Letters and a Fellow of the Royal Society of Literature. She lived in Roundstone, County Galway until 1961 when she moved to Boughton, near Faversham in Kent, where she died at the age of seventy-six. Of her work Virago publish *Mary Lavelle*, *That Lady* and *Farewell Spain*.

EL MATADOR

SOUTH DUBLIN COUNTY LIBRARIES

CASTLETYMON BRANCH LIBRARY

TO RENEW ANY ITEM   TEL. 452 4888

Items should be returned on or before the last date below. Fines, as displayed

in the Library, will be charged on overdue items.

5 - 7 ᶜ08		
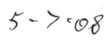 07. APR 09		

Published by VIRAGO PRESS Limited 1985
41 William IV Street, London WC2N 4DB

First published by William Heinemann Ltd, London 1937

British Library Cataloguing in Publication Data
O'Brien, Kate
Farewell Spain.
    1. Spain—History—Civil War, 1936–1939
—Personal narratives
I. Title
946.08′092′4   DP269.9

ISBN 0-86068-696-5

Printed in Finland by Werner Söderström Oy,
a member of Finnprint

Cover illustration is a detail from 'A View of Avila',
by Mary O'Neill. Reproduced by kind permission of
the artist.

CONTENTS

ILLUSTRATIONS

INTRODUCTION

WHEN in 1922 Kate O'Brien, aged twenty-four, travelled to Bilbao in the northern province of Vizcaya in Spain to take up a post as a 'Miss'—governess—in a prosperous Spanish family it is certain that she did not know she was to experience that country as a major influence in her life and future work. As she says in *Farewell Spain*—

> I was pleased in my roots with the unexpected Spain I had found—and glad to the extent that I would not realise for years to have opened up acquaintance with a country I was to love very much . . . I was in this queer melancholy town of my own choice, and for a limited time . . . I have remembered nothing much, nothing of great general or personal interest from that lost year, but I see now that though smudgy, it was a more indelible year for me than many . . . I am glad to have had it.

One feels that the slow gradual impressions received by Kate O'Brien during her year in Bilbao—daily impressions growing into familiar knowledge—were of infinite value to her.

She had no doubt taken the decision to go to Spain in a spirit of youthful restlessness. After taking her degree at University College, Dublin, she had worked in Manchester in the foreign languages department of the *Manchester Guardian*, had taught for a short time at a convent school in Hampstead and had visited America. In Bilbao her charges were a young girl and a still younger boy, José. She would later talk about this child and his lively intelligence. Thirty years afterwards she received a letter from the mature José. He wrote:

Dear Miss Kitty I wonder if you will remember me I was your pupil some years ago—how many? And since then I believe we never wrote each other though I heard sometimes news about your splendid success in the field of Letters. As a matter of fact I must say I read some of your books, *Without My Cloak*, *The Last of Summer* and found them full of interest, passion and good english. (My poor english was taught to me by you!) But then . . . I found at last the famous *Mary Lavelle* which I was looking for since years ago. You can imagine with what a tremendous anxiety I went through the pages and the vivid scenes of life in 'Casa Pilar' at 'Cabantes' near 'Altorno'. The book is really fascinating. And for me it was, still more, because a whole world which slept in my memories, for years, woke up and dreamt again as in the golden times of adolescence. Thank you, Miss Kitty, for bringing to life the dear shadows of my youth! . . . I finished my studies of both engineer and lawyer. Then went into politics and got mixed in the tremendous civil war. I was condemned to

death by the Reds and saved life by miracle. Was appointed
Mayor of Bilbao; rebuilt the city after the battle (Altorno
was half destroyed) Then became under-secretary of
Industry; and later ambassador in Buenos Aires for three
years . . . I am not one of 'Spain's Great Men' as Juanito's
father wanted but I did for my country all that I
could—and hope still to give her more, when she needs
it . . .

After her year in the 'queer melancholy town' of
Bilbao she returned to London and married Gustaaf
Renier, a Dutch journalist. On the marriage certificate
they both declare themselves to be journalists. This
marriage lasted barely a year, and she left to live in
Bloomsbury and to take a secretarial job. She had
always thought she would write, and her first play
Distinguished Villa had a tremendous success with great
critical acclaim—though its run was shortened by the
General Strike of 1926. However this opened the door
for journalism and she contributed articles and stories
to various periodicals. For some years she worked on
her first novel Without My Cloak which was published on
her thirty-fourth birthday in 1931. This was a story of
Irish bourgeois life set in her native city Limerick. It
was awarded the Hawthornden Prize and the James
Tait Black Memorial Prize. Her second novel The Ante-
Room published in 1934 was set in the same milieu. In
1936 in Mary Lavelle she first wrote about Spain in

fiction. One may take it that her description of Mary's reaction to Spain and the Spanish way of life had its roots in her own experience.

In the novel as Mary Lavelle travels by train through Castile from Bilbao to Madrid Kate O'Brien describes the Castilian countryside.

> Afternoon light lay over the plain. It was the third week of September and about some farmsteads peasants were still winnowing crops of rye and wheat. Men in suits of black cotton straightened themselves to see the train go by, and sometimes a boy waved his wide straw hat. The land was blond, unbrokenly; its fairness stretched without pause or hurry to meet a sky so far away and luminous as to be only in the most aerial meaning blue. There were undulations, there were valleys; but within this spaciousness the breaks they made were like sighs which alleviate meditation; hamlets were so buff of roof and wall as almost to be imperceptible in the great wash of gold; roads made lonely curves across the quiet and bridges of pale stone spanned shallow rivers. Here a shepherd called his goats for evening milking; there a bell rang for a village funeral.

This was Castile as Kate O'Brien saw it and to which she was to return at intervals during the rest of her life.

Farewell Spain, first published in 1937, although inspired by the outrage of the Spanish Civil War is not really a political book, though it was banned in Franco's Spain, and Kate O'Brien herself was forbidden entry to

Spain until after 1957. It is a book of reminiscence, of nostalgic pleasure, of regret for something perhaps never to be experienced again.

She does however express indignation that the Spanish Republic with its *Frente Popular* (popular front) should have had so little time to prove itself before the revolt of the generals. In 1936 the common political attitude in western Europe was vaguely left wing, and even could be said to favour the theory that the hope of political and social progress in the future might lie in communism—a theory shattered by the later realities of the Spanish Civil War, and still later by the progress of western Europe towards the Second World War.

This book of Kate O'Brien's echoes the sentiments of thousands in western Europe at the spectacle of Spain tearing itself apart. This was 1936, early 1937, when the cause of the elected Republican Spanish government seemed clear cut and simple. Young men from many European countries travelled to Spain to join the International Brigades in defence of the Republic. Germany and Italy under Fascist regimes sent aid to General Franco, Russia was reported to be sending help to the Spanish Republic.

The German atrocity at Guernica was yet to come, when this defenceless market town, traditional seat of the Basque parliament, was bombed by German pilots. Yet on the Republican side there were the appalling experiences of a loyal Republican Spaniard like Arturo Barea, or George Orwell, wounded in the throat while fighting in the International Brigade, both having to flee from Spain in escape from communists fighting for the same cause. Even with the German and Italian support for General Franco and Russian aid for the Republic the war had all the cruelty and violence of a civil war. The English and French governments decided on 'non-intervention', and the foreign aid received by Spain came from the extreme regimes of Fascism and Communism.

In a spirit of nostalgia Kate O'Brien writes in this book of her travels in Spain before the Civil War. Even in the most superficially un-'Spanish' northern towns the impact of Spain is strong and surprising. In western Europe we have had the influence of French and Italian culture—we are familiar in some degree with their literature and art—but Spain itself has seemed cut off from the general experience of western Europeans. In England in childhood we all learn about the marriage of Mary Tudor to Philip II of Spain, and then after Queen Mary's death the Spanish Armada sent against England in the reign of Queen Elizabeth I and the great English naval victory, but subsequent Spanish history is more or less a blank to the man in the street, and Spain has generally seemed apart from northern Europe. She did not, like other European countries, experience the expansion of ideas in the nineteenth century, and was neutral in the First World War. W. H. Auden's poem emphasises this separateness:

> On that arid square, that fragment nipped off from hot Africa, soldered so crudely to inventive Europe;
> On that tableland scored by rivers . . .

I first travelled to Spain with Kate O'Brien in 1935. From Coruña and Santiago de Compostela we made our way through Castile to Segovia, Salamanca, Avila and Toledo.

One's first experience of Spain can be astonishing: I speak as a painter and of landing at Coruña in 1935. The clatter of the language—certainly in the voices of the women, the *animacion* and seeming muddle, the swarms of beggars, the mutilated, all were new and alien and sensational. A child with only a stump of an amputated arm holding a saucer in its one hand and soliciting pesetas. The legless men on wheeled trollies, the occasional beggar who would draw open his shirt to reveal what appeared to be a terrible wound. It was said later that General Franco shut them up in institutions. This is probably true, as in later years one did not see such sights in Spain.

The deep chill of the churches as one left the burning heat of the streets, the savage expressionism of the figures of Christ crucified, and the overdressed and

theatrical Madonnas with glass tears upon their faces—
all very foreign to me as a northern Catholic used to the
smiling gentle Gothic statues of France.

And *Cante Hondo*—Flamenco—at its most unself-
conscious—a boy turning a corner singing a snatch of
this alien melody—if it could be called melody.

And then the bullfight: a controversial subject that
seems more questionable nowadays than it did then.
One can, while making no comment, point out that this
is another example of how Spain has stayed in the
atmosphere of the past. At this distance one feels it to
be rather more suitable to the Middle Ages than to
what we consider our enlightened and compassionate
era, though it is easy to be censorious at a distance—
away from the burning sun, the general excitement and
the intense drama.

Kate O'Brien has caught all this—the idiosyncrasy
of Spain—in this very personal book, a mixture of the
experiences of several journeys. She was a most individual traveller combining wide reading and knowledge
with a lively interest in the accidental event, in the odd,
amusing and sometimes exciting encounter. We are
given the most vivid immediate reactions of a very
perceptive temperament; somehow the essence of Spain
is here.

In her account of the Escorial she shows an early
interest in the complicated character of Philip II, a

subject she was to return to in her novel *That Lady*, published ten years later. This novel brilliantly analyses the contradictions and intense passions of the King, and his relationships with other people; a work of imagination which somehow convinces that this was Philip. She writes with freedom and feeling about actual historical events in the lives of Philip II, Ana de Mendoza and Antonio Perez in this novel which is regarded by many critics as her best work.

In her description of Avila she writes of Teresa of Avila, foreshadowing her monograph on Teresa published in 1951. Her account here is full and detailed, and the later work enlarges on the subject, and in it she quotes from Teresa's simple and lucid description of her mystical experience. This, in the time when the Inquisition was all powerful in Spain, was accepted by her various confessors and spiritual directors.

Later Kate O'Brien was to write:

I have felt lonely this last week because I have not been in Avila. Had I not had this really hellish 'flu I was plotting to get to Spain—to see them in Avila indoctrinate and receive their new doctor of the Church—Saint Teresa of Avila. You would have to know Avila as well as I do to understand how surprising and unemotional this great occasion might be. The Church will have laid on everything for the occasion, and Avila will have been filled with great and important strangers, but Avila itself, the town I know, will be taking the whole affair with a curious kind of coldness. That is why I would have liked to have been there. I would have liked to have heard all the thundering in the cathedral—and then have walked along the Ramblas and then turned back and looked the other way, north, down to the convent of the Encarnacion where Avila's greatest citizen spent twenty years in which she learned not only to live through every kind of physical and spiritual torture but whence she fled, witty and sane, and shaped in every way through mad suffering for the great work she was going to do.

(Irish Times, October 6 1970)

For many years, after the Franco ban was lifted, Kate O'Brien travelled in Spain. Most of these visits were solitary returns to the country she loved, but there were more formal occasions when, for example, she lectured in Valladolid during an Irish week at the University in 1972, and in this and other earlier visits she made the acquaintance of many Spanish writers, publishers and journalists.

She stayed one cold spring at the Hotel Jardin in Avila and wrote late into the night. Remiquio, the manager, would add to the warmth of the central heating by bringing up to her room what she described as a primitive dish of burning charcoal. He would knock late in the night to remove it before she went to bed. Remiquio himself became her friend. She would spend the occasional Sunday with him and his wife and their two little daughters, Conchita and Milagros, at their house on the outskirts of Avila. The two children would come in from Mass spick and span, removing their white gloves. Later on Remiquio would write and give her news of his family. Once he enclosed a photograph of Milagros on her first Communion day—in veil and wreath and long white dress; first communicants look marvellous in any country but in Spain the ceremonial dress is even more striking. In his letter Remiquio wrote that this photo had been taken of Milagros 'on the day on which she first received the Bread of Angels'.

In 1967 in *Hibernia* Kate O'Brien was to write:

The Spanish spirit is clear and isolated—in all its great expressiveness: from Gongora to Lorca, in Goya and Picasso, Unamuno and Ortega—in Belmonte and Manolete and even in young Jose Antonio, the Falange founder, who died too young to understand or control what he had started. You find an unchangeable Spain in the errors and mysteries of terrible Cardinals and terrible Kings—was ever a country more unlikely in her governors, her autocrats?—just as you find it in a witty shoe-shiner in the Puerta del Sol, in the tired handsome waiter who remembers you down in the Calle de Toledo, in the desperate young poet from the Calle del Carmen who may be in gaol the day after he has a drink with you.

Let us however, quote Kate O'Brien's opinion on the question of the end of Franco's rule, the restoration of the monarchy and the return of Spain to democracy.

I have been thinking about this imminent restoration of the monarchy to Spain. Since Franco first began to moot this idea—saying so obligingly, that he in his good time would give Spain back its never officially cancelled monarchy, I have astounded and indeed angered some of my friends by suggesting that, from the point of view of Spain itself, and *not* of the top class, the little Caudillo did not have such a bad idea there. Because the monarchy as constituted when Alfonso XIII bowed himself out in 1931, was already merely a symbol, a top knot to decorate what was an old-fashioned but thoroughly bourgeois and open form of government—a government which was conventionally elected into a conventional Cortes, and under which, in principle at least, there was freedom of speech, freedom of publication, as of religion and of irreligion. That the corruption of wealth and landlordism and of an overwhelmingly wealthy and powerful Church were rampant through from the nineteenth century is true, God knows; and the ingrained indifference of Spanish aristocrat and Spanish tycoon for Spanish poverty and illiteracy was always there, and seems as an immovable mass, the very rock and whole force of the Spanish problem yesterday, today and forever. But—all I mean is that under the symbolic and practically powerless Kings of Spain these evils were not hobnailed down as law, they were not authorised in the ruling of Spain—as under dictatorship they have become. With a King on that ugly, lion-guarded throne in the Palacio Nacional, the Constitution of Spain would be automatically back in the old vague mists of our grandfathers' time. And perhaps with an openly elected Cortes and the restoration of a free

Press, idealism and anger could come moving out again from their desolate hide-holes. And by degrees her poets and her educationalists might begin to be heard again. It would not be much. But it would be a start, as from way back. And any bit of a King, however expensive, is infinitely less of a mischief than a non-stop dictator.

(*Irish Times*, December 15 1969).

Kate O'Brien did not live to see the end of the Franco regime, but now King Juan Carlos is on the Spanish throne, Spain has returned to democracy, and Picasso's 'Guernica' is in Madrid.

Mary O'Neill, London, 1984

ADIOS, TURISMO

OCCASIONS of self-indulgence are rare, let moralists say what they will; and if to seek her own recollections of Spain be accounted such just now by the present writer, she must perhaps risk being regarded by others as something of a Nero.

I write indeed unashamedly as an escapist, of that which recedes and is half-remembered. For prophecy and the day ahead I have no talent and little curiosity. But death and departure attract me as man's brightest hopes have never done. So as the European *chiaroscuro* in which we have all grown up becomes its own black-out and accepts its long-drawn suicide, as doom muffles folly and the courageous turn to see what life of ordeal to-morrow brings, I still look backward, self-indulgently. The morning light, even if some of us live to see it, even if it is cheerful, will be hard; if there is anything at all in human promise,

in political struggle, it will be uniform and
monotonous. That is what the maddened world
must seek now, the justice of decent uniformity.
How impossible it seems as one writes it, and how
elementarily necessary! That it may come, after
our deluge, must be for posterity our central hope,
however obscure, however doubtful. But meanwhile if some of us can light no personal desire to
see it, that impotence must be accounted under-
standable.

Let us fiddle who can do nothing else. And
since, however the world's darkness rolls, individual life remains vivid, since faces and memories
are still precious, since there is wine still to
drink and the next cigarette remains an imperative
pleasure, we will if we are sane pursue our
constant little fads, of eating and drinking (if we
have the means), of knitting, typing, or dirt-
track-riding, of making pictures and money and
love. For there is no help for us at all in living
through this terrible day to which we have been
appointed, if it takes away our egoists' courage to
go on being ourselves. So, summoning mine, I
write for my own comfort in a vein much over-
used in the last two hundred years—but as
possibly one of the last to use it, and perhaps
deriving from that probability an especial satis-

2

faction. I write as a sentimental traveller in a country long-suffering at the hands of such. But Spain must forgive the last stragglers among her foreign lovers, as she has forgiven and condescended to the first. There will be no more sentimental travellers—anywhere. Their excuse and occasion will have been removed in that day of uniformity which we are agreed is the distracted world's only hope. The tourist is already an archaism to the right-minded, who if they still go to Russia, go only to know what the second half of the century is to be, not merely in Moscow but everywhere. They go there to view experiments and models, to examine tentatives which concern and affect us all but which may yet of course be thrown away in the rising gales of nationalism before the true shape of things to come emerges. Still, accurately informative or not, these tours to Russia are not tours with the old meaning. Their impulse is newly projected. They are a gesture towards our future uniformity, not an escapist search for novelty, individualism or the past. They are the busman's holiday of sociologists and moralists, not pleasure-trips for idle pleasure-seekers.

The latter are—let us rub it in—outmoded. And eventually even the busman's holiday will be unnecessary. If European society survives its next crisis, if science, having destroyed us, permits or maybe compels us to live again, it is to a very new sort of life that these races will be beckoned back. For science, having paid the piper, will assuredly call the tune, and those of us who have never chosen to dance to her measure may be thankful that in her hour of full authority we shall be lying still, quite deaf.

There will be no point then in going out to look for a reed shaken in the wind. The woes and beauties wrought hitherto upon the map by differences of language, faith and climate will be no longer worth consideration, for—even if they are still potential—they will be controlled, patrolled by science, the international dictator, which in any case, by air-travel, radio and tele-vision will have made all possible novelties into boring fireside matters-of-fact. The world will be flat and narrow, with the Golden Horn a stone's throw from the Golden Gate and nothing unknown beyond any hill. Antarctica, where no one lives, will be a week-end joyride, and our descendants, should any records survive to catch their eyes, will marvel at our naïve interest in our neighbours, smiling to discover that once an Arab differed somewhat in his habits from a

Dutchman, and a Tibetan from a Scot. Already in Spanish villages if they want to please a passing stranger, they do not sing a *cante hondo*—they tune in to 'Big Ben' or Henry Hall. Science, if sane survival be indeed her aim for human life, will do well to develop such a tendency, and to follow ruthlessly all the lines that lead from it to a smooth international uniformity, trampling out the romantic differentiations through which history, or our conception of it, has led us to the twentieth-century shambles. In the reconstituted world there had better be no history. Let it start bald and be allowed to grow no hair—and no teeth. Ah, how busy science will be enforcing her new health rules! Still, she can but try. Meanwhile we wait for our old, shaggy, warted world to go off in its last fit. And we count our ill-starred blessings—the junk we have accumulated and so obstinately loved and sought to increase. Temples, palaces, cathedrals; libraries full of moonshine; pictures to proclaim dead persons, quaint legends, quainter personal conceptions; songs to praise God, or a notion we had that we called by the name of love; tombs and stained-glass windows; symphonies, sonnets, wingless victories—odds and ends of two thousand silly years in which individualism, given its rope, contrived at last, after a lot of remarkable fuss, to hang itself. There will never again, let us hope, be two thousand years so untidy, or so vainly fruitful.

With these few words of self-depreciation—for we are all a part of our deplorable and guilty Christian era—with these few words to placate the forward marchers, the right-minded, let us draw the blinds again and invite our old cosiness. Let us praise personal memory, personal love.

Cosiness! As I write Irun is burning. There is a photograph in this morning's *Times* of the little plaza with its low iron seats and clipped plane-trees—the commonplace of every Spanish town. The café at the corner is a heap of broken stones. A few men stand about dejectedly with guns. Yesterday's papers showed us women sitting on the shore at Hendaye to watch the flames rise about their houses across the estuary. This Spanish war which is being waged with all the ancient Spanish will to take or administer death on terms of ceremonious cruelty—this war is only one ulcer on an ulcered world. But the individual imagination—like the racial—is highly self-protective, and although no one with a vestige of sanity can be unaware of the universal terrors of nationalisms, dictatorships and race-antipathies, to say nothing of the comic policy of sealed lips, though no one can deny that a world unable to abolish slums, unemployment, poison gas or mine-explosions, a world at the mercy of drought, floods, strikes, manipulated markets, secret treaties, private monopolies and armament competitions, is a world abandoned to evil and its consequences—nevertheless our protective dullness is only really penetrated, our nerves only really ache when that which we have personally known, that which has touched ourselves, takes the centre of the stage awhile. So for our sins we are made, and because we are made so our sins are mountains of inhumanity. But, as Mr. Salteena said about his not being a gentleman, that can't be helped now. The personal touch, sentimental individualism, has brought us to a place from which only something alien and terrible can rescue life, in destroying us who live.

Nevertheless, while China starves, Lancashire hunger-marches, educational authorities organise gas-drill for the infant class and Mussolini takes the salute from the under fours, tourists, settled in for the winter in Hampstead, Neuilly and Brooklyn, having bought new umbrellas and put their suit-cases out of sight, will mourn more than other disasters the burning of Irun. Mourn it as a sad instance which touches personal memory.

7

They saw it first on a wet morning in August.
Never will they forget their disappointment. The
night in the second-class couchettes had been hell;
they had been unable to obtain coffee from overworked, bad-tempered stewards; at Bayonne an
old woman had cheated them over a purchase of
pears. Now once past the bridge they would have
to change trains and face a horde of Customs
officers. They would be soaked to the skin. They
didn't know a word of Spanish. Would anyone
tell them the exact value of a peseta? Heavens,
did you ever see such rain?

There was apparently nothing else to see at
Irun—except just beyond the bridge, a man in
black. He was standing quite still in the roadway,
with his back to the train. A solid man of fifty, of
respectable mien, and wearing his black overcoat
slung as if it were a cape. Wearing a black beret,
too. Apparently unaware of the train and indifferent to the weather.

They saw this identical man that morning,
because wherever or however one enters Spain, he
is the first living object that catches the eye.
When your liner swings into Coruña on a warm,
bright evening, he is standing among the rocks of
the headland, his overcoat caped across his
shoulders, his beret on his head—contemplative

8

and solid. If you step on to the platform of Madrid's north station in the small hours, he is there, unchanged by a hair. Always you will see him a few paces south of the Bidasoa bridge.

He is in the forefront of every tourist's memory, that matter-of-fact, deliberating man.

But about Irun. In the café near the Quai d'Orsay the evening before the tourists had been excited—and perhaps a bit too informative with each other. Spain in the morning, the Spanish frontier. The Pyrenees, the sturdy Basques, Fuenterrabia, 'where Charlemagne and all his peerage fell.' The French road to Compostela. Pamplona, where Ignatius got his so significant wound. The Isle of Pheasants, where this and that forgotten parley was enacted between this and that forgotten personage. The flights to and fro of the Bourbons. Wellington's victories over Soult. The Carlist wars. The *pelota* game. The terrible bullfight. Or had they better see just one? Until So-and-so, still musing on the Franks, was heard to murmur, *Dieu, que le son du cor est triste le soir, au fond des bois!* Thus confounding the rest of the party and causing eyebrows to twitch exasperatingly. Was So-and-so going to prove a fearful bore throughout the trip?

Well, they got soaked to the skin. Irun is a

badly organised station. Moving between the
train, the customs-shed, the canteen and the other
train they got very wet indeed. So did their
porter, a silent, inoffensive man with light blue
eyes. Not at all a Spanish type, the tourists told
each other. They left Irun in discomfort, and
without thinking once of Charlemagne's peerage.
Indeed with no impression at all, save of the rain
and the silent railway porter. He had even taken
his tip in silence.

With no impression at all—and yet, though they
had seen Irun often since, had walked in its
paseo, talked in its cafés, taken the tram to San
Sebastian, now that it was burning they thought
first of that first exasperating morning—the man in
black by the bridge, the rain and silence. Odd
that memory of silence—because a frontier station
at the busiest hour of the day cannot be a very
quiet place. And yet the tourists, recollecting by
their cosy fires, remember it in an ambience of
stillness, and remember a bell tolling amid soaked
trees. And that was all that Spain had given them
at their first stop.

The tourists sigh, stirring their beverage. For
afterwards there was so much—they had become
so faithfully infatuated. Being genuine sightseers.
Being also of those who find life itself on any terms

of chance more enriching to the heart than the most beautiful theories or experiments of living. So naturally Spain had proved their cup of tea. And now the frontier was in flames. Toledo shot to bits, Burgos a seat of war, the Guadarramas a battlefield. Ortega, the bullfighter, was shot the other day. Bombs were falling on Atocha Station, perilously near the Prado. The tourists find their beverage undrinkable, and go to bed. But though depressed they believe, since that is the easier thing to do, that they will see their love again. Spaniards have taught them the allure and escape of to-morrow, and that it is another day. But in our time, how other? That is indeed a question. Still, awaiting its answer, it is something to have lived through the last and most stimulated decade in the history of tourism.

Something, personally. For internationally it appears to have been of little good, as the world to come will reflect with justice when the busy and self-denying populations—no longer nations—shall have removed from amongst them all the old sources of mutual curiosity, all pretexts for pleasure-seeking, all excuse for the indulgence of unharnessed, and therefore mischievous, dream.

Still perversely I repeat that I write in praise of personal pleasure. Though doom crack in my face I am glad to have lived before and not in the millennium. I am glad, too, to have lived so long after the period of the grand tour—for that would never have fallen to my humble lot—but to have known the bumpy blessings of the tourist cabin, the kilometric ticket, and the autobus. For idle travel as it has been cheaply and unceremoniously dispensed to my generation has assuredly been one of the deepest and most secret of all personal pleasures. Not, for me, idle travel, here, there and everywhere—my heart is narrow—but idle travel in Spain.

If it be permissible, if indeed it be not positively dangerous to quote Pater at this date, I venture here to quote these over-quoted words: "For art comes to you proposing frankly to give nothing but the highest quality to your moments as they pass, and simply for those moments' sake." A limiting statement, but there are those who, if they dared claim arrival at any kind of working personal truth, have found it in exactly such acceptance. Artists, whether or not they justify their classification, or even reveal at all that they carry the stigma, know themselves. They know their handicaps and, perhaps somewhat smugly, their advantages. Many of them disclaim Pater's æsthetic dictum, and can disprove it out of their own abilities and achievements while remaining incontestably artists. But for others it stands. Not that, unless they are freaks, they try to live in isolation with it, or that it yields them their whole story. But they learn, and often soberly and with regret, that it is the exaction which they most persistently understand, and they find that when it conflicts with other principles within, it overthrows them. Often wrongly or inconveniently. And the rest of us, wherever we find ourselves in the card index—are we not occasionally cross-referenced in relation to Pater's statement? Are we not visited, too, however intermittently and unrewardingly, by 'this quickened sense of life,' 'multiplied consciousness' which is the daily bread of the artist? So that, troubled and deeply pleased by the visitation, we seek it uncertainly again whenever we can?

Not as a drug. The forward marchers, who read no epitaphs and find only one sermon in broken stones, must please believe that the moony junk-counting of certain others is not, as they assess it, a vice, but rather, in its manifest non-utilitarianism, a source of strength and courage, something which, breathing over us the cold air of death—that is, of eternalness and detachment—gives brief inroads of immunity against the contemporary din, whilst simultaneously suggesting that we have patience with it. For once the Aqueduct at Segovia was a racket, a busy, practical civic suggestion, and now it is by no means the worse for that, which implication is indeed the very spine of its nobility. The spine, but not the whole. For it has become a power spanning higher than a city's need of water. No need for platitudes. Either the heart lifts at the sight of it, or it does not; either that 'heightened consciousness' is induced which can give the highest quality to a moment as it passes, or we can consider pityingly the heavy manual labour of slaves and congratulate ourselves about steel and electric power. Not that they are unworthy of our pleasure in them. It is moreover possible that two thousand years from now the soaring shell of the Empire State Building will be a nobler and more searching spectacle than it is now—if indeed such relics will be allowed to stand. Which is improbable. And as we skirt that guess let us reflect with sadness that Macaulay's New Zealander, so exciting to us all at school, will almost certainly never stand on Westminster Bridge to view the ruins of St. Paul's—(a) because in his day no self-respecting person will see the point of such an excursion, and (b) because ruins will not be tolerated, for reasons of physical and mental hygiene.

What they will do for courage then, how they will electroplate their smugness and keep their idiosyncrasies of pain and irrationality from breaking through, is their secret. You and I manage, or mismanage, as we can—snatching at straws. A book, a hand, a first-rate joke; a prayer to God, or the birth of a child; an escape into solitude or a wild night out; a fit of hard work, an attack of romantic love or of marital peace; a visit to the play; a glass of good brandy or good beer. Or a trip abroad—away from it all, as we say.

Away from it all! That is a cliché of ours which for our great-grandchildren, in their uniformed world, will only have meaning when they die. One thing we can do and they will not find possible —get away from it all. That is a strength, that weakness of ours, which, unless they are indeed to be supermen, they are likely to feel the need of. When they have tidied up everything, after our dreadful picnics, and made a Utopian Home County of the world—what then? Oh, Heaven pity them!

Unless gland control can pull off such a mon-strous miracle as poor old Christianity never even visualised, our descendants may, I fear, discover themselves to be—if they know the word—unhappy. A happy discovery, I venture incorrigibly to believe. Happy, even if bewildering, even if irremediable—save by making ducks and drakes of the Home County. And someone may even take that retrogressive measure, since, whatever else their model citizens may be, their seed, controlled, conditioned, what-you-willed, may still be supposed to be Adam's. Or is such sentimental implication painfully outmoded?

Meanwhile we, the escapists, the wreckers, still live amid our slums and ruins, sticking to our old bearded notion that life is conditioned by something never to be caught in a test-tube. While bowing a timid knee, largely out of human respect, to our glands, as lately to our reflexes, and less lately to our complexes, we children of the long shadows of individualism still hear a murmur in the shell for which we ask no explanation from without. It has a dying fall, perhaps, but we persist in straining for it. We seek the quickened sense of life, the accidents that jab imagination, for each of us believes the life of his breast to be his own and not a unit in another man's admirable sociological plan. We are in fact hopeless cases, who insist every now and then on getting away from it all.

Hence, among other good things about to die with us, *turismo*. To each his own refuge, his own holiday. Italy has been notoriously the heart-patrie of millions. So has Greece been; so have been all the Mediterranean islands. China and the Eastern seas are far flights in search of a fluke, but many have taken them. There is Mexico too—there are Africa and empty Antarctica and the dangerous lands about the Amazon. There are Ireland and Finland and the Arabian desert—all lying in their uncertain ways fallow to idle contemplation and the deep selfish pleasure of moments as they pass—all, for various unanalysable reasons of climate, history and racial temperament, contributing in some way to that individualist excitement which brings the best quiet to the heart; all insolently suggestive of life's intractable beauty.

For some of us there has been Spain. First the Spain we imagined—a place we cannot remember now—and afterwards the Spain we found. There were many surprises in that second Spain, many shocks and longueurs, and whole stretches of time when we seemed almost as inert and out of sorts as if we were at home. But somehow we went back there and went back. We got to know it somewhat—in travellers' fashion—and as we did found ourselves caring very little whether we should ever get to know any other country even one half so well. Whenever we had any money to spend we took a train for Irun, or, if that was too dear, a boat for Santander or Coruña. And crawling into those harbours—ah, the interminable, deliberate arrivals!—we were, no matter what the superficial irritations, delighted with ourselves. Though neither harbour is in the least breath-taking, even if the sun is rioting on Coruña's *miradores*, or if morning mist is pluming up from the sleepy dark hills behind Pedrosa—in the latter case, there is Alfonso XIII's ugly palace on the right—now a summer school—and many other dull vulgarities; in the former, there are some really revolting palm-trees on the quay, and nearby Sir John Moore's very ugly tomb. And in either place it is very likely to be raining cats and dogs. But we know all these things, we are old hands. Our pleasure is merely in having arrived at where we like to be. There is the middle-aged man in black, deliberating as usual and wearing his coat as if it were a cape. There are the leggy boys with sore heads, the women selling packets of burnt almonds. There are the absurd girls walking up and down in threes and fours, singing shrilly, enchanted with them-

A CHURCH AT CORUÑA

selves and their absurd toilettes. And there, as always, is the tragic-eyed porter, coming forward silently to take our bags. We are back again indeed—in the country we love to be in, the land we care for uncritically, though without illusion we think, and with eyes wide open.

PEEVISHNESS

WHERE did we land those sentimental
tourists at the end of the last chapter?
Let us say at Santander, without waste of
time. Heaven knows, enough of that has been
wasted since we last gave the creatures a thought.
'Time marches on,' as lately they have taken to
telling us with unnecessary unction in the news
cinemas. Where also we learn that the Army in
overalls marches too, and that Franco's men,
awaiting the Moors, ironically enough, in Toledo,
have held the Alcazar for more than sixty days
against Castilians. However, that is for the
moment an 'actuality,' as a Spaniard would say,
and not a traveller's tale. Time has not prettified
its steeliness. But Santander is comparatively safe
for pottering memory. Lively too. Lively enough
to make it easy for your author to mislay those
bulky tourists. Let them go therefore—they were
becoming bores. Let us be ourselves.

In short, dear readers—but will you allow the quaint appellation? A friend of mine said to me once when debunking the work of a distinguished and frosty essayist that "greater writers than Alice Meynell had called her 'dear reader,'" so I humbly take a risk with the great. Dear readers, I plunge you straight into the first person singular. I am going to take you on my own journey and narrate in *oratio recta* all that I remember of Spain and desire to see again. That is best, I think.

But my journey will be a composite one, made up of many, and without unnecessary chronological reference. The route will be a plaiting together of many routes; seasons and cities will succeed each other here in reminiscence as almost certainly they did not in fact; companions or chance acquaintances of travel will crop up, interrupt, disappear and return without sequential accuracy, and with no justification from all those useful diaries which I never keep. But their rôles will be as true, each in its place, as memory can make them—so long as no one asks for dates.

I am in Santander then, and let us say arbitrarily that the time is more than two years ago, less than three. And as I take shelter from the rain in the usual café and clap my hands for Eduardo, I hear a babble of excited English speech about me and realise with distress that the funnels dimly seen out there in the river must be those of the 'Cordillera' or the 'Reina del Pacífico,' and that yet another batch of hard-up and innocent trippers has been dumped on to the dripping wet Paseo de Pereda—holiday-makers beside themselves at being in Spain at last—"actually in Spain, my dear!"—and with thirteen summer days to spend there.

My heart sinks. For they are about to be fooled, it seems to me, and so is Spain. Here's how it is. The people who sail, tourist class, from Southampton or Dover to any of the less distant Spanish ports are mostly hard-worked wage-earners whose annual fortnight of freedom is of very great importance to them, and who are more or less untravelled for the reason that since they left school they have had only fifteen days per annum in which to do their travelling. With the increase of tourism they have become laudably adventurous—can get amazingly far afield for their money and in their restricted time. And this year they plumped for Spain. One can hear the conversations that went on, in bed-sitting-rooms and bungalows, at the agents' offices. 'The peseta is so cheap this year, and the ships are lovely. Mabel told me. About thirty-six hours each way—awfully good for you. And Spain! Such a complete change. The doctor says you need to get away from everything, darling, the children and everything. They'll be perfectly happy at Broadstairs with Mother. You know how she adores to have them to herself. Spain! What could be more exciting? We'll be burnt to cinders, I expect. Oh, then it's not so *very* hot in the north? The hotels *are* all right, I suppose? This one does seem very cheap. Oh, I think it's a marvellous idea of yours, George. Where's Toledo? Shall we see Toledo—or the Alhambra? Oh well, never mind. Spain is Spain, after all. And we'll be there practically thirteen days. You'd better buy a phrase-book, Daisy——'

Now, if they went to Broadstairs with the children, they would not think that very exciting, but they would get certain fixed benefits and pleasures with which they are familiar—the orthodox seaside satisfactions which seem to be sure-fire with most people. But when suddenly they say—"The doctor says I'm to get away from everything," and when they say: "Spain! how marvellous!" they are asking for something which, if it can be bought at all, is not to be supplied for the time and money they have to offer. They are asking admission into the poster world, a world of gamboge and cerulean blue, of singing and lounging and carnations in the mouth. They are asking to be shown at last—since the peseta is so cheap—a fantasy which they had in childhood and which has never really died.

But Spain—as perhaps everyone realises now— is not an infant's fantasy, or a poster world. It is a place of deep dimensions, of realities and stirring shadows. And Santander, to which so many innocents come flocking in pursuit of their much-needed interlude of holiday glamour, Santander is perhaps of all Spain's gateways the most prosaic and non-theatrical. It has not even Coruña's air of silly rakishness, or Bilbao's pock-marked look, made frantic by the ceaseless all-in wrestling match of greed and misery. No—it is a plain-faced, sober town of decent importance and integrity. It is the capital city of a very interesting province, it is pleasantly situated, has had a respectable history and some famous children, and has now, like the rest of Spain, its urgent social problems. Its climate is rainy and temperate, like that of Devon or Kerry; its landscape green, fertile and homely-seeming; its sea is the Biscayan, *not* the Mediterranean. The people, bred between mountains and shore, have largely the sanity such breeding gives, and its courage. They speak good Castilian, they are courteous, humorous and kind; and they and their régime are *muy español*, they would say.

But will the thirteen-day trippers say so? No, because they won't have time to find out that it is true. They will only have time in this holiday to lose their poster-world, and find nothing more real to put in its place. For unless you are very much on the spot and know perhaps a little Spanish, unless you are well prepared in advance with real information and have no obstinate pre-conception of Spain, you will find little that is novel or memorable to observe in La Montaña, as the region of Santander is called. Of course if you are a mountaineer and know your ropes, you will not linger for more than one quick drink in the Paseo —you will take the first possible bus to Reinosa or to Potes, and will make your own arrangements there for breaking your neck on the glorious Picos de Europa; if you are a reasonably alert sightseer your map will have shown you that you are comparatively near one splendour of Castile— the city of Burgos—and you'll take the bus—not the train—and spend a night at least there; if you are any kind of painter, someone will have told you of the cave of Altamira; or if you are merely a dreamer, a melancholy Jacques, an escapist, you

will fly to the lost village of San Vicente de la
Barquera and spend your twelve days watching the
sea break on its broken boats, counting the arches
of its flawless bridge, marvelling at the beauty of
its starved, wild, teeming children.

But say you are a completely random tripper,
knowing nothing except that you have landed in
Spain, and can't understand a word of what's going
on round you. You have probably booked a room
somewhere along the little beaches of Magdalena
and Sardinero, seaside suburbs of Santander which,
discovered by Alfonso XIII some years ago, won it
its still existent summer-holiday vogue. You will
find your hotel, and I am prepared to bet that you
will be agreeably surprised by it. Unless you are
very unlucky, it will be whitewashed inside and
clean and bare as a convent. There will be
running water in your room, and if that which
runs from the hot tap is not always hot, at least it
will run—and there is the sea beyond your long
window, blue-grey and friendly like the sea at
Scarborough. But if you go out and make your
way towards the Casino and bandstand which you
saw from the tram as you came up the front, if you
find the big café which overhangs the strand, there
will be only one other customer there—a man in
German-looking tweeds, disconsolately fiddling

26

with a camera. And if you sit on the breezy terrace, pouring pale tea as carefully as you can through a maddening little strainer that swings from the spout, if you marvel aloud at the empty bandstand, the forsaken beach, it may turn out that your grave-faced waiter has lived in Chicago, and can explain to you that the season is not yet, oh, not for many weeks—you have come too soon. (You are always too soon for the season in the Cantabrian holiday resorts. Never was span of time so hard to lay by the heels.) Yes, the waiter will tell you, there are people on the beach in the mornings, the local people—but the Madrileños, the fashionable, not yet. Too soon for them. The Casino will open when they come—for dancing, señorita. There is no gaming in Spain. And the band will play on the bandstand on Saturday—oh, yes, the señorita will see, a *gran baile*, *gran verbena*. A grand dance, a grand festival. On the terrace here, yes. A pity the señores came so soon. And the waiter withdraws. George and Daisy stare at each other, and decide it is chilly, they'd better walk. They walk, among tamarisks and red-hot pokers, in the little park above the sea. They have it to themselves, except for a boy who plagues them to do they know not what with the brass handle on a strange red-painted barrel he carries about. He

27

opens it and shows them curious biscuits within—
but still they do not get his drift about the turning
of the handle. He sighs, and leaves them. They
stare at the sea, and think of the children at
Broadstairs with Mother. They agree to take the
tram into Santander again, and find a warmer café,
an indoor one. As they travel in the tram they see
the ship which brought them here this afternoon
swing off now without them. Perhaps there will
be a cinema in Santander.

There is. They find an extremely luxurious one,
showing a film they both enjoyed a year ago in the
Tooting 'Granada.' They enjoy it again. They
enjoy their dinner too—they are frantically
hungry by the time they get it—ten o'clock. They
enjoy their bottle of red Rioja, and congratulate
each other on its cheapness. And afterwards,
emboldened, they walk down to the café over the
beach, and drink liqueurs, and talk to the un-
occupied waiter who was once in Chicago. Far
off, as they talk, as they watch lights flicker from
sardine boats in the bay, they hear a boy's voice
singing a wild, extraordinary song. They do not
know that it is *cante flamenco*. It saddens Daisy,
irritates George.

But the next morning is fine and hot, as fine
and hot as it was three summers ago in Ilfracombe.

Do you remember, George? And there are people on the beaches—as the waiter said there would be. And George and Daisy get into their beach-robes and go down there, too.

From now on their twelve days depend entirely on their personalities. If they have initiative and can somewhat control self-consciousness they will find at the end of those days that they have, in fact, done a number of really interesting things, and discovered a segment of the real Spain to replace their fantasy one. If they are merely observant people, not hedged by prejudice, again they will have learnt much and been much entertained by that best of all spectacles anywhere for the good looker-on—normal life, human life, being normally lived by people whose customs and characteristics are fresh to our eyes, but whose natures are not alarmingly varied from our own. But initiative and powers of deliberation are not necessarily the two things we infallibly pack, I think, when we set out haphazard and excited for two brief weeks that are to be vivid with immediate pleasure, picturesque thrill, and the brilliance and exhilaration of brief, precious holiday. So for the most part I am inclined to think—and I have talked with many tourists in Santander—the fortnight on the Cantabrian coast is a failure, and

29

when the trippers crowd back so eagerly to the 'Orinoco,' two unlooked-for things have usually happened to them—they have been disappointed in their innocent search for holiday delight, and compensatingly have been reinforced in their unfortunate national smugness. Two bad things— the second worse than the first. So when I see them storm down the gangway from their liner, when I heard their eager, new-arrival voices in the Café del Boulevard, I am saddened for them and for Spain.

Tearing shrimps out of their pretty hides now, I listen to the chatter of this new batch. I don't like shrimps much—though once I used to like catching them—but here in Santander they are almost de rigueur with apéritifs. Sevillanos tell you that they are better in their town than in the north, but the reason why the *camarones* of Santander are world-famous—and Eduardo says they are—is because a visiting bishop, entertained by the mayor of the town in the fourteenth century, found himself able to eat a large quantity of them with pleasure and without arrière-pensée. Whereupon he blessed their spawn for ever. Now, messing my fingers with this sanctified sea-fruit and still uncertain whether they are worth a bishop's blessing or my trouble, I listen

to the plans of the new arrivals. Some of them—
young-looking, with cropped heads or with
plus-fours which will please the local señoritos,
who have a fancy at present for that unfortunate
kind of trouser—some of them are going to take
lectures at the summer school. That is a good
idea. The lectures are good and internationally
comprehensive, and they will meet so many Swiss
and Germans that very soon it won't matter to
them at all that they are in Spain. Some of the
others are going to "bask, and get as brown as the
Spaniards, and hardly ever come out of the lovely
warm sea." Another has a sketch-book handy.
One of the men thinks he might learn to play the
guitar. All except the students are after glamour,
as they understand it. And all want to see the
Consul. Yes, we must find the Consul.

That is a recurrent mystery of foreign travel.
What do the British always want with their
unfortunate Consul? The Consul at Santander is
indeed a most kind and courteous man, but often—
perhaps quite unnecessarily—I have pitied him.
Escorting bevies of tongue-tied damsels into cafés,
loading them on to trams; guiding dyspeptic
City men to the English chemist; buying marma-
lade for British matrons; explaining that stamps
are bought *outside* the post-office—yes, very odd—

and that Solares water is quite as good as Vichy.
A spirited child of ten might make all such
discoveries for himself inside twelve hours in a
foreign town, and in so doing begin to live its life
—but no. We must find the Consul. Do other
nationals plague their accredited agents abroad in
so infantile a fashion? Well—I'll not tell them
how to find the Consul. Give the man a chance.
This is his busy season.

A Civil Guard goes by, with rifle and yellow
bandolier. Bent and shrivelled, not a good
specimen of the wearers of that famous patent-
leather hat, but the would-be guitar-player,
seeing the other tourists smiling at him, reproves
them. The Civil Guard is a magnificent body of
men, he understands. An English chap down on
the quay—some chap who's out here for his firm
—tells him that those men, the Civil Guard, are
the only people now standing between Spain and
absolute anarchy. Everyone looks properly
impressed.

Good God! The Civil Guard has indeed a long
tradition of loyalty to the top dog, and of ruthless
courage in defending him and attacking his
enemies. But has no one told the chap who's out
here for his firm about the Guardia de Asalto,
which the young Republic found it necessary to

establish? A new body of police which, founded on no other tradition than that of Spanish manhood, might be counted on to defend the Spanish people from the preying of top dogs? Besides it is not any police force, no matter what sort of famous hat it wears, which stands between Spain and such ideas as she may have in mind to try. The complicated Spanish temperament is not at the mercy of a policeman. Its struggle is with itself, and is of the spirit. And when it has a mind to externalise that struggle, it will do so, at no matter what wild price—as we are seeing now. Would an Englishman be pleased if Spaniards visiting Manchester, eyeing the bobby on his beat, informed each other that such as he alone stood between England and absolute autocracy? Besides, 'absolute anarchy'—oh, my friend who will never learn the guitar, don't you know that that impossible condition of life would be Heaven—Heaven on earth?

I should take these gentry to see a certain lighthouse-keeper, not a thousand kilometres from where we sit. Don Angél, the fattest man in the Montaña. Walking along the coast one day, I found him seated in the sun beside his lighthouse, and I asked him if I might ascend to the lamp. A respectable elderly man—a journalist from Zaragoza he was—had just made the same request.

So up we went behind Don Angél, whose size made it impossible for us to foresee the curves of the stairs or more than one step ahead. We got out on the parapet by the lamp at last, and leant on the breast-high wall. It was a narrow parapet and Don Angél was dinged like a soft balloon between inner and outer wall. I'm no sylph and the gentleman from Zaragoza was never slender. We must have made a moderately comic turn up there on the parapet, but there was no one to smile. Don Angél is a very grave man, and he and the other gentleman fell into talk of political theory. Of which Don Angél would have none. He is an Anarchist, and as I listened to him I thought that the generous Chesterton would have felt that, in his talk at least, he was a saint. Although, for his lunatic's dream of perfection, he would apply a merciless destruction to all Spain's ages of confused and lovely culture, her indigenous and indescribable faith. It must go, Don Angél says, it must be martyred, it must be drenched in death. I summoned enough Spanish to disagree with him, but the journalist from Zaragoza only shook his head. The anarchical idea startles no sober Spaniard. And as Don Angél talked on, of decentralisation, of the elimination of authority and its symbols, of the great offences of Lenin, of the significance of any one man, and the splendour and freedom of death, I kept thinking of Chesterton, the Catholic, and of how one may believe in anarchy, as in Catholicism, because it is impossible. As a man may be a fool in Christ, he may be a fool in his brother, and if mad for the love of God, so also mad for the love of man. *Credo quia absurdum* is a tautological axiom. You do not believe in Fascism. You see it and it is difficult to be as mystical about it as the old gentleman was, who, looking at a giraffe, protested his disbelief in it. You can like Fascism if that is the kind of thing you like. But you needn't exert yourself to believe in it. Nor, for the same reason, need you believe in Communism. But, as Don Angél said, no one has seen the Kingdom of God. No human agency has demonstrated it. Therefore it may be believed in. "There will be death and blood," said Don Angél very gently. And the Zaragozan, an anxious Azaña man, appeared to agree with him.

Well, that summer Samper and the Centre were in command, and God knows there was trouble enough seething up through Spain. Autumn was to show us that. But the summer was sweet, and the Spaniards were as courteous and humorous as ever. The Basques were kicking up a fine row against the Central government about some ancient rights of theirs, and all the Basque mayors were going to jail, and everyone was on their side, and very pleased with them. But a foreigner whose Spanish flagged before long political leaders in *El Sol* preferred to read the bullfight news and to glance at the pictures in *Estampa*. One did not know that summer—or indeed, God forgive us, even when one returned in the next—that one was in at a death, or a vast, unpredictable birth. It was sweet to sit those nights outside a certain village *posada*, to hear the soft crash of waves and feel the verbena branch sweep over one's forehead, while the village boys—every night the same three or four—leant against the verandah and taught each other new *flamencos*. The brandy was Spanish and fierce on the tongue, the singing was wild, but Spain seemed very quiet, near though we sat to Asturias. '*No pasa nada*,' we thought. Nothing is happening.

And in the hotel—we laughed at fussy old ladies from Barcelona with their Catalan tales of *pistoleros*, we talked French literature with the cultivated Don Peru, we listened sympathetically when Consuelo, the most beautiful chambermaid who ever held a duster, told us of her *novio* in the Basque mountains, of his cakeshop and his mother, and of the wedding they would have next Easter.

And we argued with disappointed tourists and tried to direct them in the ways of enjoyment.

Some did enjoy themselves. There was an Englishman and his wife who thoroughly enjoyed not enjoying themselves. And there was an Irishman and his wife who were just beginning to have a marvellous time and feel completely holidayed when their relentless steamer came to carry them off. But they, of course, were not normal trippers. For one thing, they had a month or more to spend, and for another, coming from Dublin, they had friendly dispositions, and were inclined to take life as they found it. They were shy at first. Everyone, the guests, the Señora, the porter, the page-boy, the lovely Consuelo, everyone sat in the verandah and held general converse if they had nothing else to do, and this made going in and out embarrassing for a foreigner who had to run the gamut of all manner of greetings and pleasantries with no better armour than smiles, and vague 'Si's' and 'Ah's.' And Harry the Irishman said to me one day rather nervously: "Why do they always start talking about marriage when they see my wife and me?" The *"Ola! Qué tal el matrimonio?"* of the old Señora—which merely meant "Hullo! How's the married pair?" and as that sounds faintly offensive in English and not at all in Spanish—had struck on Harry's frightened ear like a fragment of a discussion on marriage. But Harry and his wife got on well with the Spaniards, and it was pleasant to see how far in gay understanding that man could go with the five or six words he bothered to learn.

They had initiative, those two. They took themselves off on picnics, to Pedrosa in the ferry, to Solares, to God knows where. They made tea, if you please, in the maize fields and eucalyptus woods. They sat in taverns and learnt from men in overalls how to drink wine from the *porrón*. They went to the circus with the 'Señora' and me, and often still I hear amusedly Harry's voice as he praised to the old lady the limousine which she had hired for the expedition. "Chrysler *coche*—very *bonito*." They went to dance at the Casino. The elusive, mythical-seeming season, which Harry had ceased to believe in, was just beginning when they had to leave. They spent a day larking round at a village *romería* up in the mountains. (That is an all-in, go-as-you-please celebration of a local saint. *Romería* means pilgrimage.) They bought a tiny suit of blue overalls to take back to their little son. I helped them to buy it, and I hope they have it still, though they might not like to see their son in it now. I fear that Harry would never be on the side of the Army in Overalls.

They and I went to a bullfight together. I had never been to one till then—had never been able to make up my mind to go. *Death in the Afternoon* was in my suitcase but I had not read it—nor did I read it for a long while after. This fight was only a *novillada*. Also one of the *espadas* was a woman— Juanita de la Cruz. For the timid it seemed the easiest possible kind of bullfight. No horses. Small bulls. A woman among the matadors. Ruth, English and seventeen, begged me to let her come, too. I wondered what her mother, a very dear friend, would think. Nowadays, however, that is a quaint sort of wonder. I agreed that she should come.

I had never read anything about the bullfight then, except in *The Plumed Serpent*. When in Spain hitherto I had refused to go to one. Well, we went, Harry and his wife, Ruth and I. I remember sitting in my place before it began, and wondering very miserably what on earth had possessed me to come. And hearing Ruth murmur to herself in soft wonder as she looked about at all the sunlit tawdry—"I really *am* in a Spanish bullring."

It was a bad fight actually, though Juanita acquitted herself very well and three of our party became very feministic and worked up about her.

But there was a lot of silly nonsense and one young matador disgraced himself. Difficult to believe from that afternoon's experience that one would want to see another *corrida*. Harry didn't. That was definite. He took a sportsman's view of it, and by National Hunt Rules or what have you he dismissed it as silly and brutal. I was interested and perplexed from the word 'Go!' Ruth was quiet and, I suspect, made uneasy, but her imagination surrendered, I guess, while she held debate. Harry's wife was taken out of herself, was excited and thrilled and amused too, exactly as if she were a Spaniard. Wanted the explanation of everything, and cheered Juanita like mad. She had to go home on the eve of the big *feria* of five full *corridas*, and was very angry about that. I hope that she remembers her one *novillada* still and how disgusted Harry was with the brutality of the three ladies of his party. Well, they went off in their liner in due course—"Adiós, el matrimonio!" I was sorry to see them go. I wonder if the rainy, non-flamboyant Spain they found was any permanent compensation to them for the poster Spain they had come seeking?

The theatres are sometimes worth attention in the north of Spain. When Madrid grows too hot to be profitable to players, some of the first-class companies move off to the temperate coast, and I saw a delicious performance in Santander of Benavente's *Lo Cursi*. It is one of his earlier plays and admittedly dated *comédie des mœurs*, but in varying disguises the weaknesses he tilts at in it are carried through the generations and its flow and grace and unemphatic malice must be forever enchanting. Another play of his, *El Pan Comido en La Mano*, I was unable to criticise because, as it was new and still unpublished, I could not read the text beforehand, and the extremely naturalistic style of playing gave my slowness with the language very little chance. It was a more severe and emotional piece than the early, lovely satire. The acting of both seemed beautifully smooth, if somewhat too restrained and Du Maurierish.

We had musical comedies in Santander that summer, too. I remember one, or rather I remember sitting through one. An imported thing translated into Spanish which had been a riot in Madrid all the spring. It was as boring as musical comedies are. The situation seemed to strike some chord of association with *No, No, Nanette*, but alas! the tunes did nothing so consolatory. I only mention it in justice to Santander, as such diversions may be, for all I know, one of the attractions of the place. But give me its comfortable new cinema where they break the movie in the middle—as Gielgud broke *Hamlet*—and let you buy delicious ices from pretty little boys. There's a shadowy café-place in that cinema, with a fountain and with vast sofas on which *novios* whisper to their marvellously lacquered *queridas*, their sweeties, who were all blondes, oddly enough, when I was around.

But memory is growing bored in this unexceptionable town. It is time to get away from the tourists and the excessively lively *paseo* that stretches so wide and long between harbour funnels and tall, miradored houses. Time to get away from that confounded bandstand. There's no denying that Spaniards are wolves for noise. They never have enough of it. Which is curious, considering how strikingly quiet and low-spoken they are, taken man by man. (Not woman by woman. The women of Spain are natural rowdies, asking their pardon.) You'll never catch a Spanish man making meaningless noise, just for the pleasure of doing so. One reason for that may be that you'll never see him drunk; they are the most incredibly sober people—but when several or a few Spaniards are gathered together, there'll be a din created somehow, or they'll know the reason why. They don't make it—they cause it to be made.

Bands, tram-bells, whistles, motor-horns, accordions, women—and now their ubiquitous loud-speakers. I believe there is hardly a tree left in Spain from which a plague of an *alta voz* is not suspended! They are lunatics on radio. It is very, very hard to get them to be reasonable about it, without causing them great pain.

But no. I never heard an 'alta voz' in Santillana. I will arise and go now. (And please don't mistake me for a 'ye olde' fan, an arty-and-crafty, a putter back of the clock. No, sir. I'm all for modern conveniences—just as Spain is. But towards radio I feel as I do towards good plumbing —I like it in its place, though actually even there not as much as I like good plumbing.)

The plumbing is all right in Santillana, if you know where to find it, and have a few pesetas. But even if it weren't, Santillana would certainly be forgiven. Indeed, that town would have to be forgiven if it hung *alta voces* all round the sanctuary of the Colegiata. I wish I had taken Harry and his wife to Santillana—though architecture didn't seem to interest them, and the place is just nothing except a rainy, crumbling, filthy museum of romanesque and renaissance building.

The bus leaves the Paseo in Santander. It stops

43

in front of the monument of Concha Espina, a
distinguished and now aged daughter of the region,
whose celebrated novels I am always intending to
read. I like her statue, anyhow—it has seen me
off on many a pleasant jaunt. There is another
terrifying statue further down the *paseo*—the
memorial of another novelist, Pereda, a vast fellow
of the nineteenth century, one or two of whose
books I have had the hardihood to buy. He wrote
regional novels of the Montaña, and Spaniards still
regard him as a great novelist, I think. He was
muy regional, they say proudly. I'll say he was
and I'll make a guess—from my wide knowledge of
a few heavy pages—that he moralised too much, that
he overdid his regionalism and that he was sentimental. His statue is good fun, however. He
stands way up on a big hunk of granite Montaña,
all rough and realistic-like, and round this
uncomfortable hillock crouch the fruits of his
pen—bearded peasants, weeping girls, birds and
sheaves, fishing nets, reaping hooks, very old
women. All in granite. But there are many
equally interesting statues scattered round Spain.

My bus sails past Pereda now. Good-bye,
Santander. Like the girl in the song, I know where
I'm going. Through your lovely, modest province
to visit your lost jewel.

LA MONTAÑA

AND as I go I shall say a few words, well or ill-chosen, on methods of travel in the Peninsula. Words of advice, I mean. For long, main-route journeys one must naturally take the train. And the trains are all right. Perhaps they are not so fast as all that, but they serve. They are roomy and have fine, big windows. You can get good meals on the trains—good, that is, as railway meals are judged anywhere. And do not think it waste of time to travel by day. It is never waste of time to watch the Spanish land-scape marching past. Even if the weather is very hot, travel by day. At any cost it's a pity to move about Spain in the dark. If you sit still on the shadier side—the trains are very rarely crowded —you won't die of the heat. And even if you do, your last sight of earth will have been very noble. But the conductor won't let you die. At every stop he'll fetch you the coldest, loveliest beer you've ever gulped. But you must offer him a cigarette, and indicate that you would be honoured if he would smoke it with you in your carriage and talk with you a little. For among the well-bred peoples of this peninsula there is, in everyday intercourse, none of that 'Colonel's lady and Judy O'Grady' *embarras* that still goes on in other quarters of the globe. So far as one can make out there never has been in Spain. Never mind the trouble that exists there now—the class war. It is indeed a class war, and no error. But its cause, its causes, have always been vigorously living too, side by side with this other thing, this natural ease which every individual feels in the company of every other. The wars, injustices, miseries and delays which too long have maddened Spain have never impinged, as it were, upon this deep individual sense of pride and its complementary courtesy, nor would it ever strike oppressor or oppressed that they might do so. It is a difficult thing to explain, but so are many Spanish paradoxes, which nevertheless remain true. Still it is as well for the socially inhibited Northerner to be prepared for the straightforward politeness of Spanish porters, washerwomen and newspaper boys. I once saw a very distinguished English female don nearly choke with stuttering embarrassment when an English countrywoman, providing an extempore meal during a car breakdown, asked her "If she wouldn't like a nice bit of lettuce to her tea?" Why that good idea should be so remote from the understanding of any healthy English scholar I don't know, but there are people who cannot, without grave risk, be even midly surprised. So be warned—if the dirtiest and most illiterate old man in Santiago de Compostela (and he'll be dirty and illiterate) takes your bag from your lodging to the bus, at parting he will take your hand and shake it warmly and kindly in good-bye. That is, if he likes you. And no matter how exquisitely elegant you may look, he'll shake hands with you and pat your shoulder—if he likes you. If the *botones* of your hotel ('buttons,' 'bell-hop') sees you sitting bored in the empty verandah, he will come and sit with you and tell you interesting things about his life at home and his funny old grandmother, and will ask you questions about life in England. And if—as once actually happened to me—you are distressed by some news in a letter just collected at the Poste Restante, and are so indiscreet as to sit on a bench in a park and shed tears, a woman selling sweets will sit down beside you, give you a kiss and thrust a packet of burnt almonds into your hand.

But to return to my views on methods of travel.

For distances that can be covered in two, three, or even four hours, always take an autobus in Spain. For one thing, they go all over the place and they're cheap. Most of them are quite comfortable, and, like the trains, they are rarely crowded. You'll strike up amusing acquaintanceships on them, though of course you'll do that on the trains, too. But in this very matter of going from Santander to Burgos. As the crow or the bus flies, it is, as far as I remember, an affair of three hours and about eighteen pesetas first class. Ten shillings. By train—well, I've forgotten the price, but the crazy mileage you cover makes it a great deal more—and it takes all day. Nine hours—or ten, I think. You jolt away down, hour after hour, to an astoundingly uninteresting place called Venta de Baños (Inn of Baths). There you get out of your train—but *not* to take a bath. I can't imagine that anyone was ever so blithe as to take a bath at Venta. You spend two or maybe three hours in a bedraggled little garden café outside the station. (That café and one petrol pump are the whole of Venta.) There is certain to be a wedding party going on in the café. You take photographs of the whole party, by request, and write down all the addresses of the photographed. When this amusement palls you walk over to the station and

THE CATHEDRAL, BURGOS

re-consult your kindly porter about trains for Burgos. But he shakes an amused head at you. You try the *manzanilla* in the station canteen, but, after a bit, abandon it to the flies. You ask for the key of the '*señoras*' (or the '*caballeros*,' as the case may be). A senior official in gold braid crosses the line with you, key in hand. It will not turn in the lock. Some lesser officials arrive to advise. Some women arrive to assist. Some children have a try. Your porter tells you proudly that the children are his. Just as the door of the '*señoras*' is burst open, your train sails in. A mercy actually. You get to Burgos at dead of night —too late to see those lovely girlish spires rise lightly from amid shivering trees.

Meantime, as I counsel, my bus is rattling on. Up and down hills, through villages bitterly ennobled by centuries of starvation, over the river Paz, where delicious trout are to be caught, they tell me. The fields of maize look mostly dull and ugly, as cabbage-fields, with their repetitions of rose-curves, never look, but here and there, sloping oddly to the sun, they seem like fields of blue swords. Eucalyptus woods climb the hills gracefully, and groves of umbrella pines stand stylised and composed, all ready for John Nash. Rainy clouds race in from the north, from the sea; away ahead, west and south, the teeth of the great Picos glitter snowily.

The domestic architecture of these Cantabrian provinces is one of Spain's minor triumphs. Anyone travelling by road from Irun to Oviedo, or for that matter to Vigo, must be impressed by the beauty, harmonious variety and functional fitness of the older farmhouses, manors and cottages he will pass. Basque architecture has the most excellent mannerisms, and here in Montaña, where the weather is of the rainy, uncertain kind that is good for pasturage and mixed farming, how sane it seems to have kept faithful as the parish church to romanesque strength and sturdiness, alleviating it practically—since the sun does often come out and must be used and enjoyed—by purposeful suggestions of the sixteenth and seventeenth centuries; balconies, arcades and hooded courts. How faultless in these villages, against the grey, blue-grey and blue-green of the land, against the dead buff of the *Parroquia*, is the cottagers' centuries-old knack of mixing bluish whitewash and whitish blue! There are farm gateways to be observed in this region, there are cottage-porches overhanging *solanas*, which are so right and beautiful that, seeing their age and that inevitably they must soon be replaced, one groans in anxiety.

For here in Spain too, and necessarily, they have the building fever, and have it as badly—I use the word with precision—as everywhere else. They are building deplorable houses all over the Peninsula— and even where they are building fairly good ones, they're not so hot, if you get me. We talk a great deal about functionalism nowadays, as if we had discovered it—God help us!—when all we are doing is to snaffle it. We think that a boot-factory erected in Vladivostok in 1936, granted that it looks and works exactly as a boot-factory is expected to, should be just as perfect a thing if erected in Torquay, did they happen to require a boot-factory there. We divorce the idea of function completely from its external conditions. And so we hope to internationalise, uniform and, I think, strait-jacket the world. God help us! Eighteenth-century Englishmen knew a good deal about the function of a house, for England. So, for Castile, did the feudal and renaissance Spanish lords. So do many twentieth-century Americans, and no doubt, if the world hangs on awhile, some more good ways of building houses for special conditions will be found. But I believe that there must be a limit to the number of ways in which a house, shop or garage should be designed, and so I dread the consequences of allowing peaceful regions all over the globe to be startled out of their traditional good sense by armies of mass-producing gimcrackers, who will blithely take away from the timid and the innocent in one generation conceptions which have stood up gently to hundreds of years, while giving them in return a few notions which very likely would be rubbish anywhere, and ten to one are rubbish as and where applied.

These people of the Montaña could very well build their own new houses now, as their ancestors did, if they were let alone. Not slavishly imitating, but carrying on in their own terms, without affectation, the Montaña idea of a suitable house. But there is not a vestige of a hope that they will do so. Horrors are springing up everywhere—so well-disseminated are all our rotten new ideas —horrors and hybrids without health or steadiness or a vestige of grace or rejuvenation. Things made out of every kind of absurd brick and tile, brought from God knows where to the land of granite and sandstone.

And now we are passing through Torrelavega—a little wild industrial town in a wide, wet valley. Practically owned by a Belgian firm which extracts some chemical or other from the river-bed. The Belgian firm has built houses here for its Belgian clerks and foremen. To make them feel more at home. Funny little rows of flat, thin houses, of purply brick with slate-coloured shutters. Exactly such small flat houses as you see from the train on the drearier outskirts of Brussels and Antwerp. Houses built to front neatly on a neat street in a neat little country. They look exiled and wretched here in this muddy, fertile Spanish valley. Torrelavega itself is a poor and desperate place, but it is strongly built, its big square is comfortably arcaded, its workmen's cafés are vast and warm. And I think that in winter, when rain sweeps across this open stretch and plane-trees thrash on roofs, the Belgians, slipping into their slight little houses out of the mud, must suspect that the wild Spaniards, in their old shabby, thick-walled houses, deep-porched and deep-windowed, are warmer and more secure than they.

Anyway—we'll be at Santillana in a minute, where no one has laid a stone upon a stone this many a day.

ROMANESQUE AND NEOLITHIC

SANTILLANA DEL MAR lost all interest in the vulgar world about two hundred years ago, I should think, but I saw the makings of an extremely topical row there once.

A little priest, on holiday from Madrid, was strolling about one afternoon, looking at the architectural monuments, by which I mean looking at every piece of masonry in the place. I had some conversation with him in the cloisters of the Colegiata, the parish church. He was a very little man, young and pale, with thick spectacles. He told me something of the existent confusion in Spain in regard to the enforcing or not of the Republic's Law of Congregations which was promulgated in order, among other things, to remove all their teaching rights from the religious orders. This law had seemed severe and sudden to many anti-clericals on grounds of pure expediency, he said, as Spain had no schools, no text-books and no teachers ready to take over the work of the nuns and priests, and education, managed badly enough in this priest's opinion under the monarchy, was now in a state of chaos. This in spite of much laudable energy on the part of the Republican Left Government. Azaña had, in fact, had to ignore many failures and delays in executing his drastic legislation. Now under Lerroux and the Centre Government, and with negotiations opened with the Vatican, there was considerably more laxity in enforcement, and clerical hopes were rising for some amendment of the law. But meanwhile the confusion was immense, and was rousing impatience even to reaction among anti-clericals who earnestly desired that *someone* might be permitted to teach their children the ABC. "Paradoxical things are happening in Spain, as always," said the little priest. "In many ways this education affair is a very great comedy."

Later I saw him walking up and down in the street. He was waiting for his bus. There is a very poor rough café on the corner of that street—the only café in Santillana. At this hour of the evening it was crowded at all its tables by smocked peasants, lorry-drivers and artisans in blue overalls. Some of them at a table outside the door were

talking with unusual loudness, as if *at* somebody.
A second's attention showed that they were
talking, not ribaldly, but angrily about the little
priest, who continued to walk up and down, the
width of the lane away from them. A big overalled
man, very powerful but also very weary-looking,
stood up and shouted directly to the priest, who
turned, crossed over to him and asked if he wanted
him. This angered everyone at the table, and
some at other tables. No, no, they shouted, they
didn't want him. Torrents of very passionate and
no doubt very insulting Spanish broke from several
men. The priest walked away, but as he had to
catch his bus, could not walk out of their sight.
They continued to discuss him furiously. I could
not understand what they said, but they were not
drunk, as a tourist new to Spain might have
assumed. A Spaniard is almost never drunk.
Politically most of them were probably anarcho-
syndicalist, and this evening, perhaps because of
some news in the papers or for some reason of
local grievance, or merely because they were tired,
this placidly pacing soutane, this imperturbable
little symbol, got on their nerves more acutely
than was normal. They continued to rave and I
thought the priest looked nervous now. He
certainly didn't look pompous. If he was wearing

the garb they hated, well, there was no help for
that, his restrained uneasiness seemed to say—
and perhaps indeed any minute there would be no
help for him. As a looker-on I felt anxious, and
said as much to a woman in the door of whose shop
I was standing—but she smiled. As she did so,
the big man and another young fellow, followed by
a few less purposeful, rushed suddenly and really
frighteningly at the priest and grabbed him. It
looked very like being serious gangster-stuff, and
I heard the priest say: "Well, what is the matter,
my brothers?"

He said this furiously, like a man enraged.
Nothing of the saint in his voice, no sweet oil on
troubled waters. And yet he had the wit to say
'my brothers,' not—as a priest from habit might—
'my sons.'

The two big men were shaking him, and everyone was shouting. The priest shouted too. "Come
on—what is it? No need to break my arm."
Somehow, still in the clutches of the two, he
managed to push his way through the rest of the
crowd, ignoring them. "Say what you have to
say. Come on." They marched him a few steps
down the lane, still shouting. But he shouted too,
and in a few seconds they let go of him, warming
up to dialectics and needing the freedom of their

hands. When they came to the end of the lane they turned as by one accord and came back, still arguing. Before they made another turn their Spanish gravity had returned. All three were masked and quiet—normal Spaniards. They spoke in turn now and wagged their heads slowly. Every few steps they halted, as Spaniards do when they walk and talk. Their faces were intensely serious. Then the priest's bus arrived. He had to skip down the lane to it. *"Adiós,"* his two companions shouted, and he waved at them, his skirts flying. *"Adiós, padre,"* all the rest of us shouted, and the two men went back to the café table.

I was interested. In the unmistakably earnest anger of the men, and in the terrier-guts of the little priest. Perhaps he was very cunning, perhaps he understood his foe—but I think he was just manly, and in the centre of his heart perhaps, if not in his nerves, unafraid of life or death. Anyway it was an interesting round, and went on points to the Church.

And if it had gone much further it wouldn't have taken a feather out of Santillana, which was built for feudal ructions and must have seen many an all-in brawl.

It would be pointless to describe the place in

factual detail here. Every guide-book explains the
crumbling armorial bearings over every door; tells
you which building is the eleventh-century convent
of Saint Juliana (after whom the place is named);
tells you that it is the town of Gil Blas, whose inn
is still to be inspected in the square. It is still an
inn, and a very good one, greatly improved, I
should think, since Gil Blas' time. It is there
you'll find the afore-mentioned good plumbing.
You'll be able to buy little arty bits of Spanish
pottery there too—if you don't mind their price.
Altogether the *parador* has toned down, I should
think—indeed, in some ways it's so refined that
you'd almost believe you were having tea in
Grantchester, honey and all. Such is the good
influence of *turismo*. But it really is a decent
inn, and if you have read Gil Blas you'll like to see
it. It's a lovely house, with a cobbled hall where
your horse can wait while you have tea in the back
garden. And about the famous novel—your guide-
book, if written by a Spaniard, will tell you that
the Spanish translation, done by the Jesuit,
Francisco de Isla, is better than the original of
Le Sage. I can't take sides in that controversy,
however, as I have read neither version.

López de Mendoza, first Marqués de Santillana,
was a scholarly courtier-poet of the first half of

the fifteenth century. Fitzmaurice-Kelly says that
he was also a 'shifty politician.' He served a king
who was also a poet, though not as good a one as
he—Juan II, father of Isabella the Catholic. It
seems to have been a time of literary preciosity
in Spain. Santillana himself was apparently an
innovator and an initiator, and is said to have more
or less introduced the Italian sonnet to Castile.
But the three or four of his poems which appear in
the Oxford Book of Spanish Verse reveal him as a
light and gracious singer, somewhat individualistic
and of a Heine-ish turn of humour.

One way and another, then, the name 'Santillana'
has good standing in Spain's past. But the town,
which will no doubt have crumbled completely
before Spaniards forget the song about "the
milkmaid of La Finojosa," is nevertheless a greater
possession than the poet.

It stands in a green, wet valley. The hills about
it are not impressive and the sea which it claims in
its full name is invisible and some kilometres
away. It consists of two narrow streets and a
bedraggled square. There cannot be in the whole
town more than seventy houses, but they are all
palacios. It is built of that pale buff sandstone
which gives Spain such an unfair advantage
architecturally. No stone could be more beautiful,

or more felicitously suited to the romanesque manner which France sent over the Pyrenees in the twelfth century and which achieved indigenous perfection in its new place. Three or four of the *palacios* were still kept up, when I was last there, by wealthy Spanish families who come there sometimes—I suppose to shoot. I cannot think of any other recreation they could find for miles around. One house is owned by an Austrian Archduchess, a relation of Alfonso XIII, and very comfortable she has made it for herself. The other *palacios* are tenanted by villagers, whose mules and oxen are very well stabled in the great stone entrance halls. I do not know who their landlord is, or if there is, or was, a twentieth-century Marqués de Santillana.

The Renaissance laid gracious hands on this curious feudal settlement of grandees. It caressed the strength it found, coaxed and embellished it. For all its creativeness it chose here mainly to conserve, to carry on, to add without senselessly taking away. A lesson another vigorous age might ponder with advantage.

It found almost nothing to improve in the Colegiata, which stands out clear and simple at the bottom of the hilly longer street.

The descent may be difficult. If it has been raining the cobbles will be slippery as well as bumpy. The children will all accost you if you look foreign. They'll ask for cigarettes and for two pins they'll make fun of you. You may meet a team of oxen coming up, and have to sidle against them like a brave bullfighter. A mule may unexpectedly swish his tail in your face out of a magnificent front door. But you will descend and long before you do you will see the façade of the parish church. It is of the same stone as the *palacios*, it is '*románico puro*' and if you don't like it—then there is exactly nothing to be said. But if you do like it you will agree with me that here—more demonstrably than almost anywhere —functional rightness is beauty, beauty is functional rightness. In the old, wide, regional sense. For this is a church, but not for Baptists or for Irish Catholics, or for a Cardinal Archbishop. It is the parish church of a small feudal town and it was built in the days of faith, not many hundred years after Pelayo, nearby at Covadonga, had driven the Arabs back for ever over the Cantabrian mountains and had begun the history of a Christian race. It is founded on simple theology, on the Catechism —not on hysteria or inquisitorial fanaticism. It is a church for men's daily use, designed neither to inflame nor to alarm them. Its architectural mode suggests patience and mercy.

LA COLEGIATA, SANTILLANA DEL MAR

Within, it is dark, and its arches have each an individual irregularity which puzzles modern builders, I believe. The proportions are without flaw. It has a dim but good-seeming retablo and another altar piece which the sacristan holds in such high regard that he keeps it covered, except to show to tourists. It was the gift to his home-town of a local boy who made good in Mexico in the late nineteenth century. It is a low relief of religious figures done in beaten Mexican silver and is atrociously ugly.

That is all there is to say, outside a guide-book, about one of the small jewels of Christianity, except that it is open all day every day for those citizens of Santillana to pray in who are not yet Syndicalists or, like the saintly Don Angél, Anarchists. And you would really need to be very sure of your political crank if you could set fire to the Colegiata.

It is an easy walk here from feudalism to neolithic life. The caves of Altamira are not much more than a kilometre away. But it is uphill, so we'll take the bus.

There are two caves. You pay three pesetas, I think, to be shown through them and to visit the little museum. The guide has by now shown me through them so often—I have taken this one and that one to see them—that he begins to suspect I am a formidable authority on neolithic man. He is incidentally an excellent guide who can answer questions and whose information, though always the same for each party, varies in expression from occasion to occasion. It is not patter. He loves his two caves, and has taken trouble to understand why the learned, and the curious, find them exciting.

The first, which he takes you to second, on the principle of reserving the better thing, is a vast display of stalactites. Very drippy and dank. The state or someone has illuminated this dwarf forest here and there with coy little red and green lights. Everyone loves this cave and tells the guide that it is just like fairyland. He is never bored by hearing that. I think he thinks so himself. Arthur Rackham himself never thought up so vile a setting for the little people. Myself, I even prefer Hollywood's 'wood near Athens.' On my last three visits to Altamira I refused to go into the fairyland cave, much to the distress of the guide. But I really detest it and as I'm not a geologist I don't see why I need induce geological nightmares. I prefer to sit on the one little bench on the top of the hill and think up theories about the twenty-thousand-years-dead painter of the other cave.

That is dimly and cautiously lighted, because if the Neolithic Leonardo, going one better than the Florentine, managed to mix his three colours so that they would endure for twenty thousand years on the wet walls of the inner earth, his fame may well have been helped, the experts think, by the chance that his frescoes have lain a small eternity in unventilated darkness. So they are not flood-lighted—there is only one small bulb in the inner cave where they are—and you must peer and grope until you are used to the dimness, and must follow the guide's flashlight accurately—he moves it about at rather too great a speed, I think—if you are to see the animal pictures decently.

As far as I remember there are six animal forms painted on the low ceiling and uneven wall of the cave. They are done in three colours, black, red-ochre and brown, cleverly combined with the lovely buff of the surface. The figures, bisons, stags, and horses are approximately life-size, and are painted recumbent and in action. They are full of individuality and the technique is of elimination—observation whittled down to record essentials. Experts cannot decide whether they are the work of one man or of many, but intuition apprehends a personal, isolated inspiration in the idea and its execution. No one knows how the colours were made. But there they are—the beginning of painting, and setting for it a high standard indeed, but hidden ironically, and perhaps for immortality's sake fortunately, from all the eras of painting, and all the schools, until now.

This cave, so accidentally discovered, is an immeasurably precious possession from about a hundred points of view. Its value is so documentary and pure that, certainly, no one will ever be able to think up a reason for destroying it. Anthropologists, historians and all kinds of experts exult in the flood of deductions in which it engulfs them; painters straighten up and feel jealous and stimulated, and the honeymoon couples beam at the guide, and think it all very odd and irrelevant, and that the animals are in fact rather funny.

But the sentimentalist—I speak for myself—always comes out of that cave in a condition of broody inertness, a condition bordering on pain of some kind. Feeling unsociable—like a homeless, evicted troglodyte. Pondering the accidents and blisses of initiative and genius, and the arrogant irresponsibility of the processes of life and time. So when the rest of the party come out of fairyland she is glad enough to mount the bus and depart in gloom from Altamira.

SWORD OF PELAYO AND
BONES OF SAINT JAMES

ASTURIAS, like Wales, was the principality traditionally presented by its king to his first-born son; like Wales, it is very mountainous and has a wild and beautiful sea-coast; like Wales, it is rich in regional spirit and in coal-miners. Again like Wales, it once held out alone and desperately against an invader who had taken almost the whole of Spain—held out, drove him back south of León, and, as I have said somewhere else, initiated Spanish history. That invader—the Moor—never returned within sight of the cross of Covadonga until Spanish officers marched him up there in October, 1934, to shoot at Asturian miners.

Hannibal himself might have refused to give battle in central Asturias. In fact, it is impossible to imagine how or on what spot any action was fought round here in the ninth century. A different matter nowadays, of course, with aeroplanes and gas, but there can be few pieces of ground between Astorga and Campas where two companies of men could stand level for a hand-to-hand fight. However, Pelayo, the Visigoth king, had Our Lady on his side, and calling the Cantabrian men about him, for God and Saint James he rode at his enemies and sent them scuttling down the south side of the tremendous Asturian mountains. For which great feat he lies nobly buried with some of his kinsmen in a holy grotto which has an open view south to the cross beyond the gorge which marks the peak of the great victory. A stream of pure, glacial water gushes out of the rock below the grotto and never fails. Some of the pious say that it gushes miraculously by Our Lady's favour, and has miraculous properties. I know nothing of that, but only that it is delicious. As you ascend the long flight of steps to the grotto this sparkling jet shoots past you, and at a certain point a little boy will hand you a glass of it, for which you give him a penny or two. You'd pay champagne price for it if you climbed those steps on a sunny day. The boy will watch you eagerly while you drink it, and when you have finished will tell you that you will be widowed twice, or four times, or six times, according to the number of gulps you take. I swallowed mine in one—to his bitter disappointment. He did not seem to think that there was any possible interpretation for such coarse behaviour.

Mass is said every day in Pelayo's grotto, and one tall candle, which takes exactly twenty-four hours to burn, is lighted every morning before Our Lady's statue. So that if you pay a peseta for one and lay it at the end of the row of waiting candles and count them, you can know on which day yours will be mounting guard.

The Basilica which the nineteenth-century faithful saw fit to erect on high ground at the top of this charming, high-flung village is admittedly unfortunate. Neo-ogival is peculiarly out of place in a region celebrated for the enduring beauty of the little 'mozarabic' chapels which sprang up in many of its villages during the ninth and tenth centuries. 'Mozarabic,' variations and remnants of which are still to be found in many parts of Spain, is a pleasing, simple form of architecture, evolved in the earlier days of the Moorish invasion by native craftsmen who having worked for the conqueror returned to their own places and grafted some of his mannerisms—the horseshoe arch, for instance—on to their own then crumbling Roman and post-Roman buildings. 'Mozarabic,' though

earlier and more modest than romanesque, pre-
figures much of the good sense of that style, and is
not to be confused because of its queer name with
a later vulgarity called 'Mudéjar,' a most unfortunate hybrid evolved in Castile and the south by
Christianised Moors.

The hotel at Covadonga is rather grand and very
quiet. As I sat on its flagged terrace and heard the
soughing of the trees and the running of the water,
as I admired for the millionth time the Spanish
sky and tried to count the points of the coronet
of mountain peaks which, because I was nearly as
high as they, did not oppress but only stimulated
me, as I watched the village drowsing in the sun,
and drank the cool, thin air—I had a deep desire
to stay where I then was. The peace of the place
seemed impenetrable that morning. But it was
once a battlefield, and in that very summer, though
Samper and his Cabinet made little, outwardly, of
stories of gun-running round Gijon, the food for
powder was getting itself ready, even while it
hacked away at coal in the pits of these very hills.

I knew nothing of that, however. The rising
smell of the trees was delicious. So was lunch.
I wished and wished that I could stay awhile in
Covadonga.

But I was leisurely bound for an agreeable place

—Santiago de Compostela. And perhaps following the 'French road,' for all I knew, the great pilgrims' road of the Middle Ages, which ran between St. James's shrine and the Pyrenees. Many interesting things came to Spain along that road. Civilisation came actually—to a country too harassed by perpetual battle with the Muslim to evolve it for itself. (Help for the battle came, too, from Charlemagne and from Saint Louis.) Romanesque silted in along that road; political and legal science came; knowledge of lettering and illumination— the Irish theologians brought that. No doubt the Wife of Bath contributed something in the way of gaiety to Galicia, too. And the monks of Cluny eventually brought the new French building vogue which was to find expression in the Cathedrals of Burgos, Toledo and León. Literary fashions came, of course—the *chanson de geste,* and the troubadour craze.

But although that is very fine, and although it was very interesting to be arriving for the first time in 'the Rome of the Middle Ages' (so called by the Galicians), life there began rather irritatingly, and indeed mediævally, for me and for my companion. We were attacked by bugs.

I must take this unfortunate episode carefully now, in justice to Spain. Because I take very hard the nonsense ignorant people talk about the prevalence of these creatures in the Peninsula. No doubt all over the world, wherever there is poverty and its unavoidable partner, dirt, there are plenty of bugs. Where there is heat as well, they are likely to thrive. But the Spanish people, all of them who can raise the price of soap, hot water and whitewash, are thoroughly clean about their dwelling-houses, their bedding and floors and upholstery. Or so I, in a fairly long knowledge of them, have always found. And I had never, in Spain or out of it, seen a bug until this sad evening in Santiago.

I was particularly exasperated, because my companion had not come from Covadonga and Santander, but from Coruña off a boat, and she was absolutely brand-new to Spain. Moreover she had asked me, timidly enough, about the danger of bugs, and I had eaten the face off her, as we say in Ireland. I had never seen a bug in Spain, I repeated, and I begged her not to annoy me with that topic. And then—a woeful night in Santiago, and astounding red blotches all over one, and at dawn the sight of an ugly little creature crawling. Well, I would take steps. I would keep silence. Perhaps the newcomer had escaped. But no— when I went to her room I found a figure of woe and frenzy who had had no sleep, and claimed that she was scarlet all over with bites. She certainly wasn't. Still—Spain was repaying my loyalty rather badly, and I was miserable.

It was impossible to imagine that our affliction could be blamed on the house we were staying in. Our rooms, the bathroom, the dining-room, were models of monkish cleanliness, and we felt in fact desperately guilty towards the "señora," for we decided Coruña, and Coruña alone, was to blame. We had brought the devils with us on the bus from Coruña.

I have not lingered on Coruña in this reminiscence, because, in spite of its being the home-town of Don Salvador de Madariaga, I think it is a rather boring place. Although we encountered some charming people there—and that, dear readers, is how we think we got our bugs. Because on the night when we wanted lodgings in Coruña we found it in the howling thick of a mad 'feria,' and packed to its top mansards. No rooms anywhere, anywhere, anywhere. We marched about through the demented crowds, escorted by a charming porter, who captained two bare-foot fisherwomen, who—God help them in that heat!—carried our bags. Resolutely again and again, to the porter's polite surprise, we refused rooms of the 'interior'—because they had no windows whatever. On a sweltering summer night. At last an acquaintance of his spoke to the porter. A very grave, quiet man. Yes, he had a hotel, with rooms. He would take us there. Yes, his rooms had splendid windows. Off we all went with him, delighted. His hotel was called, say, 'El Mundo Occidental,' or such. We wondered how we could have overlooked anything so stately.

'El Mundo Occidental' was a tiny little flat in a raging slum. Sure enough its rooms had marvellous windows, looking out on to a decayed, wild, dirty street with proud Renascence doorways. Its beds were clean; so were its floors; there was hot water in a curious little bathroom, rather awkwardly crowded with the toilet gear and intimate clothing of a large, young family. We were delighted that the porter had met his friend. He gave us a lovely, simple supper, *cocina regional*—and the newcomer was in heaven. She had been at the point of death through hunger. We made many friends in that little dining-room that night—the proprietor, his wife, his cousins from Madrid, and his Michael Angelo babies who rolled about the corridor naked. And, to please us as much as they possibly could, they got us 'Big Ben' on the radio.

74

We must have got the bugs there. The house
was very old and dark; it was surrounded by
slums of the noblest kind. Anyway, they were my
first and last Spanish bugs so far—and I think
neither I nor the newcomer bears any grudge
against 'El Mundo Occidental.' We were very
happy there—and one bad night in Santiago was
no great matter. For the very next morning we
found a smart Japanese insecticide in a shop in the
ancient Rua del Villar—potent stuff in tins that
made a popping sound as you ejected the powder.
An embarrassment, that sound. With windows
wide open it was impossible to take a mere
unnecessary precaution at dead of night without
betraying to the newcomer next door your tran-
sient distrust of Spain.

However—that's enough about bugs. I only
mention them so as to protest against the legend
that they are a pest in Spain. Idiotic!

Of all the towns that I know in the Peninsula
the two that I would be most content to stay in for
a long time, and between which I should find it
hard to choose, are Avila and Santiago de
Compostela. (You simply couldn't live long in
Santillana if you have a spark of human nature in
you. There isn't a newspaper shop within miles,
and the café is a most bleak and comfortless

place.) But Avila and Santiago, taking their teeming beauties for granted for a moment, are both, though small, alive and rowdy. Both have good shops, though I think Santiago wins on that, because, a university town, it has good bookshops, and I didn't notice a bookshop in Avila. Both have good cafés, though Avila's are the more amusing, I think. But as to that, Mary—the 'newcomer' of this narrative, who since its events has travelled far and wide in Spain, and now knows it better in many ways than I do—Mary tells me that the cafés are closed in Avila in the cold spring. And I suppose that for a Northerner, Santiago would have it on climate. The plain of Castile three thousand feet up, the snowy Gredos, granite Guadarramas. It might perhaps be rather much. 'Nine months of winter, and three of hell,' is a tag one is tired of hearing about the climate of this and that Spanish town. But in regard to many of them, the 'three months of hell' is nonsense. Castile is not hell in summer. It is very hot, but it is not hell. In fact, if you have low blood-pressure, it is very like heaven. But then I'm crazy on Castile. Santiago, in a valley of fertile Galicia, and with the sea very near on two sides, is rainy and temperate. Rather colder than England in winter, I should think; rather hotter in summer than a good

English summer. But definitely a catarrhal, uncertain place. Not dramatic in its weather, like Avila. I'd certainly like to see Avila in snow. As soon as I can buy a fur coat I'll go and see it. And by the way, if this war is allowed to continue through the winter, if it is to go on being encouraged and lazily ignored, what a war of utter agony it will be—on that high, bare, tragic plain. But let us leave that. I seem to keep getting on to uncomfortable topics—first bugs, then the Spanish war. Suppose there were no war, or suppose by the time they stop their war, Avila is still alive behind her Gothic ramparts—would I prefer to live in Santiago? Yes. No. Avila is gold-coloured —dead gold, and so, in summer and early autumn is all the infinite, gentle world about her. The air and blue sky are Castilian, and she is only two hours from Madrid by train, three by bus. Anything that is near Madrid is near my heart. But Madrid is dead. They are bombing her straight to death. So for one reason and another I suppose I'll choose Santiago—for if her lively neighbour and traditional foe, Coruña, is a rather boring place, there is Vigo just as near, and charming shabby Pontevedra. There is Finisterre, and there are all the long, wide *rías* of the coast. There are guelder roses everywhere, and over every peasant's house a florid vine. In summer all Galicia is a garden. Yes—for the moment I am choosing Santiago.

In spite of the fact that people are always saying that its outer communications are disgraceful, Santiago has no idea, I think, that it is cut off from life. In fact, life, its own everyday life which it assumes to be not unlike that of other towns, though rather more pleasant than theirs, of course —for men are Spanish here, too, and spiritually self-contained—keeps Santiago humming along. There are no trams, mercifully—and only a cripple would need them in that sized town. Some jolty buses come in and out from other places. There is a train which jogs at a rather affectedly slow pace to Pontevedra and Vigo. Some people have cars, and the rest have their legs. And though they are very glad to see the tourists, they've been seeing them since Blessed Saint James himself was brought for burial. Meantime, they're not a museum, in their own opinion. They've always been an extremely important place. They are the Rome of the Middle Ages. They are used to the situation and very glad you like their wonderful town.

It is largely of granite—dark grey streets deeply arcaded and breaking into oddly slanting little squares, full of sudden light. But the Cathedral, its great, stupendous heart, turret or dome or façade of which you see wherever you turn, is buff-coloured, of sandstone. Externally at least, this cathedral is, in its class, the most beautiful building that I have ever seen. The Renascence Hospital across the square from it is more perfect, more of a piece, but it is a small thing, ideally designed for a straightforward materialistic function of mercy. The Colegiata at Santillana is perfect too, I think, within its range, and there are buildings in Salamanca and Toledo with which it would be hard to find fault—but if your notion is to build a cathedral and to take your time over it, to space the labour out over centuries, then you are indeed putting a very especial strain on sense and sensibility, laying a million frightful traps for yourself, and implying peculiar qualifications.

Perfection, in the deft and malleable human sense, is not what is required of a cathedral. Indeed, such a result would offend against the essential conception of infinitude to be conveyed, and so by arrogance fail and win an unfortunate kind of imperfection. A house raised by man to praise God cannot be, like the circle, something upon which God Himself could not improve. Rather it must imply stupendous effort, enduring vision and then—the impossibility withal of saying what only seraphim can say. It must take its triumph, if it can, as far as Saint Teresa got in that ecstasy of which she said sadly, emerging from it, that had it lasted another second she would have understood the Mystery of the Holy Trinity. The great Cathedrals do this variously. They convey the great Christian purpose of the Middle Ages, its terrifying Christian passion and—in their greatest glory—its Christian humility and humanness.

I have seen many of the great English cathedrals and some of the French and German; I have seen Burgos and Toledo. I admit the ethereal suggestibility of Gothic, and the unearthly luminous effects sometimes of its interiors. I admit its power to seem afloat, to be on tiptoe, and that Santiago de Compostela—romanesque—renascence —is very firmly planted on the ground. A heavy-weight. But in dimension, in proportion, in the relation of subsidiary buildings to the main, in its free and excellent decoration and in the almost modesty of its baroque towers and cupolas, it seems to me to say in a particularly powerful and sober idiom, its own, all that faith could possibly externalise of its ideal. It seems to me at once the most touching and most majestic of

THE HOSPITAL, SANTIAGO DE COMPOSTELA

great temples. It has indeed at first sight a very royal and bejewelled look, but lived with it suggests much more that life is heavy, that contrition and mercy are its constant necessities, that prayer must go on though ecstasy fail, that the Gate of Glory is only one way in to God's presence, and that in His house there are humbler doors.

I may be wrong by the book in my predilection for this mighty church. Certainly I am no expert to judge its merits and defects—and I may be seduced, as I have been all over Spain, by the colour of the sandstone. But here in this cathedral and in the group of buildings which surrounds it, the seminary, the convent, the military school, the hospital—all sixteenth- and seventeenth-century structures of varying degrees of beauty, with the Plateresque hospital the queen of them—here you have a settlement of mellowed, buff masonry, beneath a blue sky and with granite and green trees for sober backing, and the result is a rightness and nobility of which no eye could ever tire.

Gautier cried out again and again in his journey through Spain about the lovely colour of its buildings. "L'ardent soleil d'Espagne, qui rougit le marbre et donne à la pierre des tons de safran, l'a revêtue d'une robe de couleurs riches et

vigoureuses, bien différentes de la lèpre noire dont
les siècles encroûtent nos vieux édifices." In
Toledo he made that particular comment, and I
think it was also of a Toledo building that he used
the word 'orange.' But the latter adjective may
have been applied to something in Andalusia, which
I do not know. But I do know Toledo, and know it
when full August sun is on it—Gautier is extremely
amusing and ferocious in his accounts of Spanish
heat—but although I agree with him about the
glorious clear colour stone takes in Spain, I am
surprised at his use of the words 'saffron' and
'orange.' 'Gold' has a more accurate suggestion
in it. Toledo is gold and buff, I think. And though
it seems well enough, I cannot completely accept
Gautier's attribution of this to the sun, or to the
infrequency of rain, as he also suggests. For if he
knows the South well, I know the North, where it
rains and no error, and where the sun, though it
can be hot, is never really torrid. And it seems to
me that the great sandstone mass of Compostela,
and even the darker, damper-seeming buildings
of Santillana have an almost Castilian loveliness of
colour—though less dramatically presented, for
they have greenery about them, whereas the towns
of the great plain rise unshaded by a leaf to a
passionately transparent sky.

To discourse on the details of Santiago Cathedral is not my intention here. Those who have studied them themselves would not thank me for my pains; those who may eventually go to see them will, it is to be hoped, provide themselves with an efficient guide-book; those who may never arrive at the 'Rome of the Middle Ages' had better not be teased by too many pages of purely personal impressions. But it would be sheer affectation not to mention the Gate of Glory—like pretending you didn't look at "Mona Lisa" last time you were in the Louvre.

The Gate of Glory, Pórtico de la Gloria, is not easy to find, as, in spite of the suggestion of its name, it is not visible from outside the church. It is a sculptured archway set a few feet inside the main doorway and leading into the main aisle. It is well worth sitting down in front of for as long as you like, if only the canons of the Cathedral would be so kind as to provide a row of chairs. It is the work of a sculptor called Mateo, of the eleventh century, whose own head you will find carved on the inner side of the central column—back to back with Moses, I think—when eventually you go through the arch into the church.

It is the work of a very great master. It is really three arches, the main one divided from the others by solid columns bearing many figures, and within itself by a slender column bearing only Moses, and at the back, as I have said, the modest head of Mateo. It is perfectly proportioned, and crowded with lovely, vivid figures. God the Son sits in the middle, surrounded by apostles, evangelists, angels, prophets, martyrs. They are all radiantly cut out in beauty—a touching and everlasting heavenly pageant. And in each extreme corner, a little out of things, a little forlorn and tattered, there is an angel of heart-breaking loveliness. If the weather is hot and the morning has been industrious, the tourist is tempted to throw all decorum to the winds and sit down on the tiles in front of the Gate of Glory.

Beyond it in the church itself, you will find romanesque darkness, very effective in a hot country which to this day has been unwilling to accept the Gothic beauty of windows in its churches. You will find great dignity of shape and mass, great peace and impressiveness, and as often in Spanish churches, a gigantic toy. This time it is an almighty huge censer, hanging by pulleys and chains and Heaven knows what from the central dome, and reaching down almost to the heads of the faithful. I have never seen that censer in action—that is a treat reserved for great occasions. But one must hope that whoever works it is in full command of it, and understands its range of swing. One blow from it ought to be enough to send several hundred of the devout straight up to the original Gate of Glory.

What else do I want to look at again in Santiago before I leave it, regretfully now as two years ago? The Park, most certainly—that gay, delightful Alameda where Borrow first met, at dead of night, a fearful bore called Benedict Mol, but which I remember full of babies and flappery nursemaids, and for its casual open-air cafés where the lemonade was agreeably bitter. The funny little museum near the café, too, where there was an exhibition of modern Galician art. "Not so hot," as Mary said. In fact, plumb bad, as she also said. (She is a painter. She is the illustrator of this book.) And on top of the wild little hill in the park the church where we found the woman caretaker helping her over-excited children to expel a flock of birds. The view of the Cathedral which you get from the long walk that circles the hill, the Herredura. The long grave Rua del Villar with its big, cool café under the arcades. The University courtyards, small and grey with academic, seventeenth-century facades, and sweet-smelling bushes. Above all, the College of Pharmacy. Only in Santiago have I been visited by a desire to be a pharmacist. The shabby blue-and-silver theatre where we saw the Italian puppets do Josephine Baker and a bullfight and the *Barber of Seville*. The flock of nightmare hens we met in the lane near the Franciscan convent. Good God! Such diseased and terrible hens! How we ran from them in the boiling heat up that stony hill ! The three, four, five little old modest perfect churches hidden away in lanes. The woman in the tobacco-shop who objected to selling cigarettes to females. The train to Pontevedra, the green-shadowed garden-stations on the way, the rose-bushes, the open *rías* and little boats, the vines that streamed down the faces of cottages. Pontevedra itself, shabby and graceful; the bullfight there—the evening *paseo* in the leafy park, and later, the procession of Our Lady through the dusk, when, preceded by bands, and children, and candles, and by such grotesque pasteboard giants as are brought out for Carnival in Nice, she was borne on her high, white brancard all around the town. The weary journey back to Santiago. The fountains of Santiago, the slanting, sunny squares. The teasing little boys who sit about the fountains. And Enrique, six years old, the type of all these little boys, Enrique who took up with Mary, as she in extreme folly with him.

86

COURTYARD OF THE HOSPITAL, SANTIAGO DE COMPOSTELA

I thought Enrique something of a pest, I must say, for all his charm. But then I'm a cranky person and not easily taken with childhood *qua* childhood. However, Enrique, much encouraged, though not by me, adopted the '*Inglesas*' for the period of their stay in his town. He allowed himself to be photographed—for a consideration. He ate ices graciously, and so on. He was certainly nice to look at. His brief cotton rags did not conceal his classic shapeliness. He was slender and yet solid of torso. His round, dark head rose quite nobly from his longish neck. His hair was black, his eyes and teeth were brilliant. He skipped about after us on perfectly made feet. He was as brown as an Andalucian. He was, I admit, an absolute baby, with no trace of the 'gigolo' in him yet. And one day I saw him look perfect. His English admirer and I were coming down the Rua del Villar when he came dreaming round a corner and was surprised to see us about twelve feet away. "*Las Inglesas*," he said, and clasping his hands together he gave a little dancing skip in our direction, which as a perfect phase of gaiety and pleasure I don't think I shall ever forget.

Mary, who was in Santiago again last year, naturally found him again. Seven years old now, he had been promoted to the profession of his

ten-year-old brother, Juanito—he was a newspaper
boy. Vociferously with Juanito and their pal
Antonio he sold *La Voz de Galicia* every evening.
He used to sell hers to Mary, allow her an hour
to read it, and then collect it to sell again. He,
his brother and his brother's pal appear to have
been her bodyguard in Galicia last spring. She
bought them *alpargatas*, jackets, ice-creams, Lord
knows what. She met their father, an unemployed
railwayman, sore-eyed, dispirited, she said, with
no trace of Enrique in him. She met their mother,
carrying their baby sister, heavy with a baby just
about to be born. She parted from the whole
gang with reluctance, I understand, and Enrique
threatened to board the Coruña bus with her and
come to England. Often now she worries about
him, in case the war will come his way—but I
tell her that he is probably profiteering heavily,
selling stop-press editions of *La Voz*.

So Rome of the Middle Ages fades from me
again, its baroque towers clear and noble in the
background and in the foreground a little smiling
boy.

THE BARBER OF SALAMANCA

IN retrospect I admire Salamanca and desire to
return there, but while I was in the place for
a variety of capricious reasons I did not truly
appreciate it.

The journey there from Santiago had been a
desperate business—occupying from four in the
afternoon until seven the next morning. In
broiling weather, and with a change of trains and
two hours' delay at Astorga at 2 a.m. However,
Spain can't help being a large place, and complicated cross-country journeys between its provincial towns must be taken philosophically. But
on arrival there and at an attractive hotel on the
Plaza Mayor, to be coldly assured that there could
be no question of coffee or of hot water until
after nine o'clock, for some mystic reason for ever
withheld—that did not help my never very
philosophic temperament towards sympathy with
Salamanca. Withal, dejected and dirty, to have to

say a sudden good-bye to a conception which had held my imagination strongly since childhood, I really got off on the wrong foot in Salamanca.

When I was ten and read the *Lay of the Last Minstrel* I took a tenacious liking to the name of the place where Sir Michael Scott got his magic— *Salamanca's Cave.* This liking stayed with me and brought a specific idea with it, or rather two ideas, a picture and an intention. A picture of a dark, small rainy place of grey stone, where it was practically always night, and where everything was done by stealth and almost as if by sleep-walkers. And an intention to see it. It is the only place which I remember when I was young being absolutely determined to see sometime. God knows why, because the above description of my fantasy, which is as near as I can get to it, strikes me as revolting now, and I wasn't, I think, overweeningly interested in magicians and their goings-on. But I liked the words 'Salamanca's Cave,' and they made me curious. 'Curious' is the *mot juste*, I think—nothing else. The curiosity stayed with me in adult life. So that honestly— I'm not trying to be whimsy-whamsy now—when I at last saw Salamanca I was quite considerably set back, superior though the bright reality is to my dank and silly notion. It was all the more

childish of me to be surprised, as, although this
town was new to me then, Castile was not, and I
ought to have realised that there would be no
chance of finding darkness, rain and sleep-walkers
in any corner of that alive and vivid region. Still
—my brain was not functioning well that morning.
It was battered—practically in shreds. For I had
travelled for fifteen hours in the company of the
Barber of Salamanca and his silent wife and
brother-in-law. They were returning from their
summer holiday on the coast, and were very kind
to us when we boarded the train. Gave us good
advice about this and that, and, incidentally, told us
to go to our unwelcoming but, as it afterwards
proved, very pleasant hotel. (I had been going to
go to the 'Bull's Head' where Borrow stayed, and
which was listed in my 1932 Spanish Hotel book
as good and inexpensive. But this nearly killed
the Barber! How did I possibly not know that that
hotel had been pulled down last May, and was
being rebuilt? But how did I not know? He
laughed till the tears flowed.) Anyway the Barber
talked all night, and fidgeted and chuckled and
talked and talked. All through the long pause in
the canteen at Astorga too—where we leant in
strange green lamplight against a wall and waited
for very bad coffee; where I remember Mary

muttered to me—in a surprising pause of the Barber's—that the Barber's brother-in-law was a Picasso harlequin. He had a masked and weary face. The Barber was physically a Sancho Panza but with none of Sancho's wit and less of his steadiness. I shall remember him for ever. I am tired already now through letting the memory of him become too definite.

Salamanca was his mania. He was just that proud of it he couldn't say! Not as an ancient university town of fame and beauty—though of course he wouldn't have a word said against a single stone of it, however old and out of date—No, Sir! But he admired Salamanca as their citizens might admire, say, Omaha, or Carthage, Ill.

Boredom is of two kinds, passive and active. The passive kind tells on one in the end, but the active is immediate agony, and leaves a cicatrice that is liable to throb again if touched in later life. I am rather subject to active boredom—but the scar inflicted by the Barber of Salamanca is one of my worst, and will never be completely insensitive. (It is certainly as bad as that inflicted by two women whom I knew in America fifteen years ago, and which still responds uneasily to my memory of them.) I have sometimes believed that I could see shadows spread under people's eyes when they

were being frantically bored. I have seen faces
age and sag under the onslaught of amiable extro-
vertism—and then I've known exactly what was
happening in the victims' agonised heads. Well,
the Barber turned night into day that night. He
told me—the others were feigning sleep, but I
couldn't because I can't keep still when I'm in
pain—he told me the seating capacity of every
restaurant and cinema in Salamanca. He told me
the names of all the films which had come to those
cinemas since their inception—and his own
opinions on them. He told me the names of all
the cafés and hotels, of all the doctors, dentists,
lawyers, chemists and shoeblacks. He told me
everyone's income, and the make of everyone's
car. He corrected himself, he recanted, he woke
his wife to get her ruling on certain statistics, he
did sums, he remembered, he recalled, he agreed
with himself. He was right—that was so, yes,
of course he was right! Ha, ha! And he began
again. In sheer delight he began again. He boasted
frightfully without a pause.

That was the night we put down. So that as
dark lifted outside from the scene which, with
certain parts of Ireland, I believe to be without
peer for beauty, as light returned to the golden
plain that I had not seen for twelve months and

exposed its morning innocence, the stillness of its villages, the peace of its scattered shepherds standing like Gothic saints among their gentle goats—I didn't care, I couldn't look.

And when the frantic business was over, when there had been about five sweet minutes of the silence and absence of the Barber, to be told—in the minimum of quiet words, I admit—that for two hours there could be no kind of reviving drink! Is it odd if I decided to hate Salamanca?

Eventually of course there was coffee. A bath, aspirin and sleep. In a lovely bed in a room with a marble floor. So that by afternoon one was able to light a cigarette, stroll on the balcony and look at Salamanca. Unfortunately some facts of the Barber's about the recent removal of the trees from the Plaza Mayor, and the why and the wherefore of it all, came over one in a muddled rush—you know how nightmares can create a hang-over. But I had myself in hand a bit at last. I refused to bother about the trees. The Plaza is lovely without them, anyhow. It is very wide, and quite square, I think. It is all of a piece, pure seventeenth century, colonnaded on its four sides, and with light, narrow balconies running along the first and second floors. All the houses are of the same height, four storeys—rather low and ample of face. The Town Hall, in the centre of the eastern side, and some other public office exactly facing it on the west, are more decorated than the other façades, but Baroque had laid its young, light hand symmetrically and thoughtfully over the whole square, which is full of Castilian sunlight. It is a most satisfactory example of civic building. A bright and inviting Plaza.

I remembered Borrow's sneers at the sinister clerics mumbling and plotting together under the colonnades. Those were the dark Carlist days, of course. And these are darker days for Spain, but the clerics seem to be well and truly muzzled now. Not much plotting left for them to do even here in their centuries-old preserve on which their tradition has impressed so much nobility. Curiously tough and engaging, that bigoted, honest fellow, Borrow. Catholic in all my blood, for years I could not bring myself to read *The Bible in Spain*. The idea of a member of the English Bible Society setting out to sell Bibles to Spain might suggest courage, but there was also too much obtuseness in it to make the record seem worth reading. However, in the end I read and re-read it. It is a shrewd and entertaining book— and yet, as the writer records with a faintly smug simplicity his conversations and friendly negotiations with this bookseller, that professor and the other priest, one has an embarrassing suspicion that, for all his shrewdness and working knowledge of human nature, his sturdy leg was sometimes gravely and unostentatiously pulled. Maybe I'm wrong. Anyway, when he was in Salamanca he had dealings with the Irish priests at the Irish Seminary —and his generous tribute to them, which sweeps him on exuberantly to toast the Irish scene and Irishwomen, comes very sweetly and disarmingly from the self-confident Bible-seller.

And that reminds me of my duty in regard to his book. I don't often borrow books, but I borrowed Borrow's *Bible in Spain*, and left it, where it might well feel at home, in a bedroom in Burgos. I borrowed it again—merely to look up something —in London. And it has disappeared again— vanished out of my flat. It really looks as if one of these days I shall have to buy three copies of *The Bible in Spain*.

In spite of the Barber, or perhaps because of him, I did not find the Salamanca cinemas up to much, or the cafés either. Though I suppose the latter were all right. Any café would serve under those colonnades with that sunny square to look out upon. And Salamancans, like all Spaniards, live out of doors, taking incessant leisurely *paseitos*, little strolls. So that except at the siesta hour, there is ample entertainment without going into cinemas. It is a widespread town, built harmoniously outward from the Plaza over the sides of a hardly perceptible hillock. The river Tormes washes past it, flowing west to join the Douro at the Portuguese frontier. All about is the open, austere plain, broken around the city's skirts and, in some of the squares, by acacia trees and lines of poplars. Almost every façade in Salamanca is beautiful, and the general tone is of buff, or of granite that is almost white. The famous Gothic House of the Shells seems at first a pretty novelty, but after a day or two one is weary of it. The Cathedral, romanesque-renascence and sandstone, like Santiago, falls very far indeed below the standard set for it by Galicia, for though from far off, from across the river, it can look noble enough with baroque tower and dome, close up its details irritate, and the bright splendours of the interior are quite shocking. There is more than a touch of the Barber's civic swagger about the inside of his Cathedral. But the big Dominican church of San Estéban is beautiful and beautifully cloistered. And they have a confessional box there— as in many other churches of Castile—where Saint Teresa confessed her sins. And the little church of San Martín is lovely romanesque.

In the University they show you, preserved now, not used, the lecture-room of Luis de León, and the guide tells the good story, that you already know, but that bears repeating—that the great poet-theologian, editor of Saint Teresa, was arrested by the Inquisition in 1572, and kept a prisoner for four and a half years while the Holy Office tried to trap him into heresy; he was released in 1576 and restored to his chair in Salamanca, and that on the day of his first lecture after his return, when the hall was packed and everyone expected some dramatic piece of self-justification—he took his chair and began: "Gentlemen, as I said in my last lecture . . ." His lecture-room is very pleasant, whitewashed and luminous, with the narrow worn benches and ledges for note-taking heavily scarred with initials of forgotten theologians. The whole University is attractive, with renascence staircases, sunny courts and whitewashed lecture-halls. And the Irish Residencia, still full of Irish seminarists, is a place of quiet grassy courts and sixteenth-century cloisters.

When I read now in the books of journalists who have come back from the Spanish war of the brave new idea of some of the anti-clericals to save the more beautiful churches and convents from

EL CONVENTO DE SAN ESTÉBAN, SALAMANCA

the anarchists—save the structures, that is, letting them have the furniture to burn—and to use them for garages and markets and so on, I am, I confess, very much bewildered. Of course, if there is to be no more praying, if that is done with for ever— then the number of empty museum churches, too beautiful to destroy, which Spain will have on her hands, will be a very ludicrous burden. But garages, markets! Oh, Heaven, how humourless people can be, how smugly blind to the strong reality behind life's great expressions! Will they make a dance-hall of Santiago de Compostela? No, no. The thing is not so easy as all that. Young men born yesterday can't be so ridiculously right when apparently all the centuries have been so wrong. They must think again about what to do with their priceless, emptied structures. Give me an anarchist every time rather than these bright, utilitarian dullards.

But let us leave Salamanca—by the same long and many-arched bridge over which a very famous son of the region departed about four hundred years ago on the first of his cynical adventures—as a blind man's guide. Lazarillo de Tormes, better known to modern Spaniards, who really know the comic characters of their literature, than the great Luis de León. Lazarillo's story, written anonymously, appeared in 1554, and was the first picaresque novel. It is very short, and in its manner of matter-of-fact, laconic cynicism had probably never been bettered. It shows the Spanish genius in one of its most successful and characteristic moods, realistic and cruel humour. I have not read it in Castilian, though I believe it must be limpid and easy reading for a foreigner, but in its contemporary English version by David Rowland, so strongly recommended by Fitz-maurice Kelly. Lazarillo is a young devil who lives on his wits, and tells his own past adventures when, as town-crier of Toledo, with a wife who is under the benevolent protection of the Archdeacon of San Salvador, he has reached his peak of bland prosperity. It is an admirably neat and amusing story and, as the authoritative Fitzmaurice Kelly says, "may be read with as much edification and amusement as on the day of its first appearance." So over the bridge with us, seeking less tricky fortune than Lazarillo, and only looking back to reflect that Salamanca is at its best in this per-spective—seen as a whole, as a shapely assemblage, a successful municipal achievement. Which it would please the Barber to hear. God be with him. And now two hours to Avila by bus. Two hours of summer evening on a Castilian road.

SANTA TERESA

THE main square of Avila has a variety of names. One guide-book calls it Plaza de la Constitución, another Plaza da Santa Teresa, a third Plaza del Mercado. On its name-plates it announces itself impartially as Plaza Mayor, Mercado Grande and Plaza de la República. I believe it has also been known as Plaza Torquemada, Plaza San Segundo, and Plaza del Alcázar. Some day perhaps a decision will be taken, but Avila—"dont l'origine se perd dans la nuit des temps," says the guide-book—is not disposed to do things hastily.

Nevertheless, when the city does decide to name the square, let us hope it gives it its only true name. Constitutions come and go, and so do republics; markets have, as Avila knows, their ups and downs. But Saint Teresa is for ever, for history and humanity so long as they remain. And she was of Avila. A genius of the large and immeasurable kind of which there have been very few, and only one a woman. Let the feminists who, anxiously counting up their Sapphos, Jane Austens and Mesdames Curie, always ignore Santa Teresa—let the feminists pull themselves together and get this square correctly named once and for all. The monument in the Centre celebrates Avila's great men, with Saint Teresa at the top, as she must be, and the only one of them the passing visitor remembers. Her legend is scattered over all the town, though with a certain Spanish carelessness and non-sentimentality. Spanish crudity too. One does not like to see her index finger in a bottle—though that represents a mere nothing, as one discovers from her biographers, of the mutilations perpetrated on her remains by rapacious lunatics and votaries of the seventeenth century. But her leather girdle, the hazel-tree she planted, a drum she had when a child, her little drinking jug—(not the pretty *calderica* which Maria de San José sent her from Sevilla and of which she wrote to the donor, before giving it away—"Do not think that because I wear lighter serge now I have gone the length of drinking from anything so lovely")—these relics touch imagination gently and make us less afraid of the strange, impassioned mystic, of whom presently we find, taking some trouble to approach, there is no need on earth to be afraid. For Teresa, who would never have dreamt of saying that she was captain of her soul, was in fact captain of all her faculties as almost no one else in history appears to have been, and was therefore able to suffer, and record, a long-drawn and awful adventure of the spirit without sacrificing a jot of her human reality and understanding.

When I was in Avila two years ago I knew little of Teresa save from Crashaw and from certain pious anecdotes heard in childhood. Some of the latter excellently characteristic in spirit even if sometimes apocryphal in fact. For instance: in the last year of her life, when she was sixty-seven and oppressed with severe complaints, kidney and stomach troubles, intermittent paralysis, ulcerated throat and an arm so awkwardly broken and set that it was now quite useless, she was on the road to Burgos in winter with a few of her nuns—about to found the last of her reformed convents. They had to go over a floating bridge which, when visible, was so narrow that to cross it in single file called for great courage and sure-footedness. On this occasion the wretched plank was submerged two feet below a hurrying winter flood. "Hinder me not, my daughters," said Teresa to the rather frightened nuns, "for it is my intention to cross first, and if I am drowned I command you not to attempt it, but to return to the inn." So she marched across the plank and all her nuns found the nerve to follow her. But once at the other side she addressed God irritably, as on some other occasions. "Strange that as I have consecrated my existence and all my labours to Thee, Thou shouldst treat me in this way." And the Lord answered: "Thus do I treat my friends." To which Teresa retorted: "For this reason Thou hast very few."

In childhood and as a girl she was spirited and exceptional. Everyone knows that when she was five she set out with her brother to get herself martyred by the Moors—but few know what she dryly narrates in her autobiography of that idea: that it was by no means for love of God but because she had decided that those who were so clever as to get themselves beheaded by the infidel had found a very cheap and easy way of securing happiness for ever. The notion of everlastingness held her child's brain. *Por siempre, por siempre* she used to murmur to herself, of heaven and hell, as she 'prioressed' over her dominated brothers. But though she liked the *monasterio* game, she had no notion whatever of playing it in earnest later on. She grew—according to herself—into a vain and romantic-minded girl, read novels of chivalry on the sly, and even wrote one, sought the company of giggling flapper cousins and imbibed with interest their knowledge of life and the world. Until her pious widower-father, worried about her, clapped her into a convent to learn sense. But here, to her surprise, Teresa still found that she enjoyed life, and the society of the nuns. For always, to the end of her days, she enjoyed society, and was rapaciously interested in people. She found no religious vocation here, however. Instead, at the end of two years she developed the first of those strange, helpless, unexplained illnesses which plagued her through her twenties. So that her father removed her from the convent and sent her to recuperate in the mountains, in the home of an old, melancholy hyper-religious uncle, who made her read St. Jerome and St. Gregory to him every evening. The effect of the fathers of the church on her convalescent nervous system was to terrify her against human life, and also against the endlessness of the world to come. *Por siempre, por siempre*, she heard again and she was a poet. So, against her father's wish, with no vocation to serve God, but simply in terror of everything real and imaginable, she fled to the Convent of the Encarnación and took the

habit. "I do not think that when I die the wrench
will be greater than when I went forth from my
father's house. . . ."

The Encarnación, where now they show you in
the vast chapel the site of Teresa's cell, and the
altar-piece carved from the wood of her pear-trees,
was in 1533 and for long after a very easy-going
and jovial kind of convent. It was overfull of
aristocratic, lazy nuns who had no notion of
obedience, and who liked to spend their days
gossiping and flirting in the *locutorios* with their
smart relatives and the friends of their smart
relatives. Also with the easy-going, hair-splitting,
heresy-hunting friars. But Teresa spent twenty-
nine years there; more than twenty of them being
an incessant struggle with illness, disillusionment,
spiritual fears and the premonitions, very alarming
and disheartening to her, of mystical experience.
She was bent on living the life she had undertaken
to live, but her standards were high, and every
difficulty seemed to be put in her way, within and
without. In the Encarnación she learnt all that
about convent life which she implied when she
wrote that, as she found it, it was a short cut to
hell, and that no father should be such a fool as to
allow his daughters to embrace it. She learnt also
so much about women that in later life she was

EL CONVENTO DE LA ENCARNACIÓN, AVILA

supreme and unmatchable in commanding them.
And in the last seven or eight years of her stay
there, when she was in her forties, she had to
undergo an adventure in illumination which every
man must explain or dismiss as he chooses.
Teresa could never explain it herself, but never
were sanity, modesty and sheer intelligence so
brilliantly exercised to attempt the impossible.
Her autobiography, written by command of her
spiritual adviser before she was fifty and before her
active life began, is a model for ever of discipline
in writing. It is short, simple, Castilian, idiomatic;
its metaphors are from daily life, its tone is
completely modest and cautious, and the writer's
patient search for exactitude gives muscle to every
line. Yet she treats of that which in her time was
not only alarming to her steady logical brain, but
with the Inquisition flourishing, highly dangerous
to her life, and which since her death has been
misused from a thousand points of view, as she
knew it would be—for she was very much against
the dissemination of talk about mystical experience,
and to the end of her life not only was sensitive
and silent about her own, but extremely severe
on other visionaries and would-be contem-
platives.

Nor will we talk of it here, who are so completely unfitted to do so. Only there is this book, her first, which dealing with an ineffable theme impossible of satisfactory solution save for those who dismiss it as completely pathological, yet for simplicity, honour, dignity and formal poise takes its place at the very peak of the noble literature of Castile.

So here, in her forties, in illness, madness, what you will—and if after reading the autobiography you can use those words conclusively about Teresa you are indeed a comfortable insensitive—her day of genius begins. Her contemplative period completed, her union with God become manageable and for ever more her own most private matter, acclimatised to her state of permanent prayer, as sane, witty and matter of fact as only the best kind of Castilian can be, she sets about her suddenly realised job—the reform of the Carmelite Order.

She has twenty years of life ahead of her—twenty years of incessant activity of every possible kind and of every possible kind of discomfort and ill-health. "This body of mine has always worked me harm and hindered me." She was very impatient of her health, as of everything that delayed her, even to the goosequills with which, at amazing speed, she wrote her books and her thousands of brilliant, witty letters. Everywhere the goosequills were bad, except those which her brother sent her from La Serna. "You'll think from my writing that I am ill—and it is only the number of bad goosequills that I use." She strikes a chord there in one who can never find a suitable pen—but, alas, her noble, spacious handwriting, exposed in the Escorial Library, shows that for once a good workman quarrelled with his tools.

The story of the twenty years can be read in many sources. But best in her own letters. During them she was everything—preacher, teacher, lawyer, cashier, politician, poet, tramp and charwoman. She was the best cook in all her twelve convents, dishing up the fish "as God ordered." Although impatient of book-learning —"God preserve you, my daughters, from being *latinas*"—she was a formidable match for inquisitor or Salamancan doctor. She was a fighter and a schemer, a soldier and a most subtle diplomat. The Papal Nuncio called her "restless, disobedient, contumacious, an inventress of new doctrines, a breaker of the cloister-rule, a despiser of the apostolic precept which forbiddeth a woman to teach." She was a communist: "Let no sister have anything of her own but everything in common and to each be given according to her need.

Neither must the prioress, etc. . . . . all must be equal." This is her eternal cry, up and down Spain. She was a feminist: "I will not have my daughters women in anything, but valorous men." Though of women *qua* women she thought very little. "Put no faith in nuns." And "It is needful to keep a sharp look-out on what these 'prioritas' strike out of their own heads." But she hit out at the friars, too. "It is to be wondered if they will obey the king, so used are these fathers to doing whatever they like." And "Pray God He lays a heavy hand on those friars." She even suspected the enemy-monks of grave crime. "Be careful what you eat in their monasteries." And she was hard on herself without ceasing: "How malicious I am!" again and again, and a thousand lamentations for this and that defect. "God make me a good nun of Carmel, for better late than never." "Already I am becoming quite a nun. Pray God it lasts." "In Avila when they tell me I am a saint I tell them to make another, since it costs them no more than to say so." "During the course of my life they have said of me three things: when I was young that I was fair to look upon; then, that I was witty; now some say I am a saint. The first two things I once believed in and have confessed myself of having given credence to this vanity; but in the

third I have never deceived myself so much as even
to have begun to believe it."

She was ironic more than pointedly witty, I
think. Her letters are fluidly mischievous rather
than barbed. But her mockery could be clear
enough. To a prioress who showed some traces of
self-importance in office she would quote the
Castilian proverb: "*falta de bueno mi marido alcalde*—
for want of a good man my husband is mayor."
To María de San José, Prioress of Sevilla and a
rather erudite woman, she wrote commenting on
some display of learning in the other's letter:
"What you say of Elisha is good, but not being
learned like you I don't know what you mean about
the Assyrians." This dirty crack has since become,
I believe, a Castilian formula for putting down the
pedantic.

She was mad on cleanliness, and on asceticism.
"From good houses, from comfort, God deliver
us!" She thought horses and saddles quite
unnecessary for travelling round Spain. Donkeys,
which were always throwing her to the ground,
were her idea. "It is unseemly to see these dis-
calced lads [her monks] on good mules." But she
discouraged all individualistic mortification, and
was strong for the rule, and for a good sufficiency
for everyone—when possible, for her houses were

extremely poor—of such food as the rule allowed.
"Do not be afraid of sleep," she reiterates to the
over-watchful, the too-anxious.

She was convivial and gay. She made up
couplets and *villancicos* for her nuns to sing at
recreation. Frequently in her letters: "I was
amused . . ." "I laughed at what you said . . ."
She teases: "How vain you will become now you
are a semi-provinciala!" When one of her convents
is enjoying some privilege she would like to share:
"God pardon those butterflies in Sevilla!" When
she has hurt a nun's feelings: "You must forgive
me. With those I dearly love I am insufferable, so
anxious am I that they should excel. . . ."

She was very shrewd and had need to be. The
ecclesiastical politics of her last decade are
bewildering to read of. "Be warned always that
a peaceful settlement will be the best. Lawsuits
are rude things." And she put fun into intriguing.
When she suspected that her letters were being
opened, the Inquisitors became "the Holy Angels,"
and Christ became "José." Reserved and humble
about her books, she was lightly vain of her
impromptu couplets and dashing off her latest—
from memory—in a letter to the erudite prioress
of Sevilla, she says: "I remember no more. What
a brain for a Foundress! And yet I assure you I

thought I had not a little when I wrote it. God forgive you for making me waste my time like this!"

Always she was noble, asking the impossible of life and of herself, preaching the most generous doctrine of perfection. "Accustom yourselves to have great desires, for out of them great benefits may be derived, even if they cannot be put into action."

And all the time, while she wrote her great 'Camino de Perfección,' her 'Moradas,' and all the noble injunctions of her letters, she was unceasingly at work, fighting tooth and nail to recall the relaxed and decadent Church to its true purpose. Unceasingly at prayer, too, by her mastery of the mystical life. She was the last great mediævalist, and though she saw the actual triumph in policy of what she worked for, she asked too much. Humanity could not give what she could, and all that she was died with her. She was the last of her kind, and perhaps the greatest. Certainly she was the greatest woman in Christian history. She died repeating "*Cor contritum et humiliatum, Deus, non despicies.*" The Church canonised her, her votaries have heaped her name with every sort of idiotic legend, and thieving friars and dévotes have torn her body dreadfully apart. After a tussle,

Saint James of Compostela held his place against
her as official patron saint of Spain. But her life
and written works endure, for those who care to
examine how great and unexpected human nature
can be. And she is the glory of Avila.

Wherefore I think that in this case even the
claims of the Republic might give way to her in
the parochial matter of naming the market square
of her home town.

"Avila," says the Blue Guide, "a un aspect
conventuel, sombre et froid." 'Froid' I can indeed
believe, though I have only been there in high
summer, but it is my desire and hope to see it
some day under snow. No town could con-
ceivably wear that decoration better. 'Conventuel'
—I suppose; the place is certainly rich in
ecclesiastical architecture. But 'sombre'—impossible, as I understand the word. For this is Castile,
the world of light. Castilian towns can look very
sober—indeed that *is* how they all look, with the
exception of Madrid. They can look ancient and
respect-worthy and sometimes, from a distance,
as Toledo, as Avila, they suggest a simply told,
unprettified fairy-tale. But they stand on a high,
ascetic plateau, their air is thin, and their sky, so
clear as to defeat all imagery, suggests, as nearly as
anything can, infinity. Under its immeasurable

arch of delicate light I cannot apprehend what the guide-book means by 'sombre.' The brilliant sadness of Castile, its permanence and patience, the touching naturalness of each town set from 'la nuit des temps' in its inevitable, sunny place— this is not sombre, I think. In any case, Avila in summer is neither 'sombre' nor 'froid.' Indeed it is very hot. But I, to my surprise and pleasure, do not find the great heat of Spain insufferable. I have been in Madrid more than once in August-September—a season when even the most loyal *madrileños* hold their town in horror—and I have been glad to be there then, feeling well and active. In this experience I appear to be alone among travellers from the north. (Read Gautier's amusing outbursts against the Spanish sun.) But I note my own reaction here, as it may be of use to other intending travellers—because at home I am anything but a sun-worshipper. I dislike and avoid sun-bathing, which makes me sick and gives me a headache. Ultra-violet-ray treatment induces irritability and insomnia, and in a London heat-wave I am limp, disgruntled and useless. Yet let me mount up to Castile in August, and provided I can be indoors from two to five like everyone else, I don't care how the sun blazes. I go about hatless from end to end of the torrid day. It is a question of the relation of blood-pressure to altitude—and certainly is a point which will affect the summer tourist's appreciation of the centre of Spain.

Avila, like Santiago, is a mixture of granite and sandstone, but in summer at least its dominant tone, to my memory, is, like that of its landscape, blond and sun-washed. Its famous granite walls with their eighty-six turrets still look a marvellously good fortification—except against enemies in the air—but they surround rather less than half the town, and that the less interesting half. All its most important monuments, except the cathedral and Saint Teresa's index finger, are without the gates. Even the main square.

The cathedral is not appealing. It is granite, and *románico-gótico* transitional. It is built into the city wall and is in fact a part of the fortifications. Within, it is dark, short-naved and lofty, and possesses a great many of those boring, second-rate religious pictures of which Spain has been so prolific and before which sacristans exact from the tourist a fatiguing reaction of solemnity. But an immense stylised sculpture of Saint Christopher, slung absurdly far up on a high dark wall, seemed as if it would be worth more effective showing. However, the Cathedral need not stay

one long. There is something brutal and thick-
seeming about it which is not elsewhere in Avila.
And outside its main door the late nineteenth
century has added a comic touch. A series of
short granite posts, between which chains are
slung, bears each on its flat top a squatting granite
lion, with extremely realistic backside turned
formidably and rudely towards the church. A most
ridiculous sequence of lions. I tried to photograph them, but alas, my photographs never come
out.

All the rest of the town is lovely. It slithers
carelessly about the sides of a golden hill and west
and south down to the Adaja. It is placed high,
but far away on every side the cold points of
mountains fence its landscape in. There are
acacias and plane-trees; children abound; there is
much noise and life. On market days the plaza
is packed and all through the afternoon shepherds,
on foot, and farmers, on mules, depart at their
leisure through one or other of Avila's iron gates,
and take their way down the hill towards the *sierra*
or the *paramera*. Leaving the tourist to cruise
about at will in the cooling, emptying town—
northward to the Encarnación, pleasant, shaded
silent place which gave such scandal to the
sixteenth century and turned a mystic into a

reformer; or west along the bare, blue-shadowed Salamancan road to the Quatro Postes, pillar-guarded cross where the five-year-old Teresa, resting on her way to martyrdom, was discovered by an uncle riding past; south-east to Santo Tomás —formidable home of the Dominicans where Torquemada sleeps and where Isabella the Catholic chose to bury her only son, the Young Infante Juan, under a sepulchre of Florentine grandeur which Spain admires immensely; northward again between the bullring and San José, Teresa's first Reform foundation, to San Vicente—the most beautiful building in Avila. Decorated romanesque. It stands somewhat apart on the hillside, arcaded, sun-bleached, with a few light trees about it. Westward from it, through St. Vincent's gate in the fortifications, the tourist can traverse a complicated zigzag of interesting and aged streets, finding the Ayuntamiento in its sober square, and the palace of the Palentinos, and the Church of San Juan, and many agreeable country-town shops, and the ornate, seventeenth-century-built church on the side of Saint Teresa's home. Southward he can pass out from the fortifications by Saint Teresa's gate on to the Rastro, a leafy *alameda* which runs by the walls and the Alcazar, and from which there is a majestic panorama over the

THE CHURCH OF SAN VICENTE, AVILA

Adaja and the plain of Castile. If the knitting nursemaids will make room on one of the benches by the edge—indeed, if it is possible to reach those benches without knocking a few swarming, hoop-bowling children over the precipice—the tourist will desire to sit on the Rastro and collect for long remembrance what lies before him. In the foreground the tower of Santiago del Rio, further off San Nicolás, still further Our Lady of the Cows. Roofs of dwelling-houses, the river; acacias and bushes of rosemary. Roads, ash-white, hardly discernible against ash-blond fields. Thin poplars, groups of farms. Empty, golden, harvested land. Strips of long shadow, movements of flocks. At the remote and dreamy edge the snowy mountain-heads. Above a speckless and incomparable sky. Nothing that can be held in dramatic words; nothing sweet, nothing emphatic. Simply a view worth a thousand journeys and which one hopes to keep in recollection always.

And when it grows cold on the crowded bench, as it does at sunset, the Paseo del Rastro leads back under the fortifications to the square of many names, where, at the far end, opposite the *románico* church of San Pedro, there are two or three big cafés. Here, with drinks and the Madrid newspapers and with a friendly, informative shoe-cleaner at his feet—admiring his English shoes, though Spanish shoes are actually much nicer—the tourist may pass an hour or two quite happily till dinner. For it is the time of the *paseito*—the little stroll—and the whole of Avila will be out, and up and down before his chair. The noise will be terrific, from *alto-voces*, motor-horns, newspaper boys and babbling strings of girls. All linked together these, in fives and sixes, dressed to kill, painted and waved, talking sixteen to the dozen. Here and there one worth looking at; once in a blue moon perhaps a beauty. But as they go, up and down, up and down, moving well on the whole, one must admit, looking them over with impartial eyes one sees that in Spain, even here in Saint Teresa's Avila, the men win—on appearances, at least. The sherry-drinkers in the chairs around, the swaggerers in sports cars, the lorry-drivers and shoeblacks, the little begging boys, even the giggling louts, would-be *novios* of these strutting fillies—all have a quality, a seriousness and individuality of face which are denied their countrywomen, it would seem. The men of Spain are related deeply to their landscape, but the women—in their florid youth at least—seem grotesquely out of touch with it. Save now and then. Save once in a town, perhaps—with luck.

Anyway, let the 'Guide bleu' see this square of
Avila now on an August night at eight o'clock and
set down if he can that it has an 'aspect conventuel,
sombre et froid.' 'Conventuel'—ah, Saint Teresa,
answer him in ironic amazement from the top of
your monument. 'Sombre'—in a blaze of elec-
tricity and radio-music. 'Froid'—yes, perhaps a
little now, though the light-clad natives do not
seem to think so. Home, then, tourist, through
the clatter, leaving it to Saint Teresa. Home, up
the hilly street to the hotel by San Vicente.
Hereabouts there is so little noise that one can
hear the shiver of the acacias. No hope of dinner
yet—but how good it will be when it comes! In
Avila of Teresa they cook as she would like them
to, "as God orders."

NO PASARÁN

I APPROACH Madrid now as never before—in
a mood of weary sadness. Frequently as I write
these casual reminiscences I feel what I
suspected when I began them—that I am indeed
a Nero sucking pleasantly at happiness given me so
short a time ago by a country now in agony. And
as Madrid, the Madrid of only one year past,
comes rippling out untidily and showily to meet
me along the dusty road from Los Pinares, I feel
self-conscious before my own sentimentality and
reluctant to go forward in search of what is lost.
For to talk now of the only Madrid I know—gay,
leisurely and *moqueur*—is as if, in the hearing of a
friend who has suffered some grievous bodily
disaster, one were to discourse of how he was before
his day of wounds and mutilations.

But though there are many deaths for her sake
now and likely to be many more, this is not Spain's
deathbed; and though the phœnix rising cannot be

said to be an unchanged bird, nevertheless Madrid, with mended and perhaps not wholly recognisable face, will live its characteristic life again—some day.

I am not a Communist, but I believe in the Spanish Republic and its constitution, and I believe in that Republic's absolute right to defend itself against military Juntas, the Moors and all interfering doctrinaires and mercenaries. And naturally I believe, as one must, in the Spanish Republic's right to establish itself communistically, if that is the will of the Spanish people. A very large 'if' with which only Spain itself can deal. If I dissent from communists in the matter of this Spanish war, my quarrel is mainly with non-Spanish doctrinaires who have 'got' communism in the all-surrendering way in which adults sometimes 'get' religion and who for the time being sincerely believe that history can be sufficiently understood, and its lesson applied, through the materialistic conception. No notion, it seems to me, could be more likely to mislead a well-wisher of Spain, but to argue against it here would be to distort the whole concept and purpose of this book. It is enough that it should be clear, as we approach the capital of the 'all-Spains,' that the writer is on the side of the Republic, of the Army

in Overalls, and of the indomitable *madrileños* who
have said of the Republic's enemies: *No pasarán*—
they shall not pass.

When I was young I was frequently given lives of
saints and such-like to read which belonged to what
I called the 'little-did-she-know' school of bio-
graphy. Dramatic irony lurked everywhere for the
writers of these books, but they were unable to
handle it. I sympathise with them now. I am
very much in the 'little-did-she-know' mood, and
as uncertain as any hagiographer how to control it.

For though Spain has long been full of portents
and here, there and everywhere for the last three
or four years there were signs of possible, even
probable explosion, few, I think, can have read
them exactly aright, and certainly when I last saw
Madrid fifteen months ago, its spirited populace,
whatever its political passion, was not foreseeing
that so soon the ultimate heroism would be asked
of it.

It is not, was not, a heroic-looking town. Its
ruins may now have forced that aspect on it, but in
normal life Madrid struck no Castilian attitudes.
It is, in fact, quite common-looking; lively and go-
ahead and much influenced, I think, by South
American notions of civic splendour. *Muy
moderno.* It is very proud of its few and ugly

rasca-cielos—skyscrapers. It has some terrific banks and cinemas and a G.P.O. which it quite rightly calls a *Palacio de Comunicaciones*. There is nothing about it of a lesser Paris or of a smaller Latin New York. Nor, on the other hand, is it an enlarged Toledo or a more majestic Santiago de Compostela. It is Madrid—sunny, alert and welcoming. Frankly swaggering with a touch naïve in its smartness. But by temperament, character and situation undeniably the capital of Spain.

Once I stayed in a hotel in the Puerta del Sol, which we are all tired of hearing is the Piccadilly Circus of Madrid. It serves the same purpose as Piccadilly Circus, of giving a centre to urban life, but it does this in a way distinctly its own, for a people who are not English. There is no spiritual resemblance between the Puerta and Piccadilly— nor much in aspect. The former is a big, half-moon of pavement filled with yellow trams, sunlight and lounging conversationalists. The houses surrounding it are tall and shabby and mostly about a hundred and fifty years old. I stayed in one of these. For ten shillings a day I was given all my meals and two rooms which had been made into one by the removal of folding doors. These rooms were floored in black-and-white marble and furnished in crumbling second Empire. They were rather like the Café Royal Grill Room, only nicer and much shabbier. I was on the second floor and my two balconies looked over the Puerta. It was a heavenly room. The brass inkstand was the shape, and weight, of a galleon. There was electric light at many desirable points, and *agua corriente*, hot and cold, in the basin. The bed was immense, the atmosphere *muy simpático*. In spite of the noise of Madrid, which is violent, I slept so well in that room that morning after morning the old goblin waiter, clattering gently through from the outer room with my coffee, startled me out of deep dreams into an attitude of alarm that visibly alarmed him. I think, kind old man, he thought I suffered from some kind of morning madness. Anyhow, he was always quite nervous when he brought the coffee—and so was I. Merely the result of exceptionally good sleeping in the centre of the noisiest town in Europe.

But if the Puerta is rowdy, the hotel was peaceful as a dream. I remarked on this one day to the proprietor. He was a very handsome man with a monkish, contemplative air. I congratulated him on the tranquillity of his house. He was fondling the head of a little girl of about six, who leant against him. "Yes, señorita," he said dreamily, "I like silence." "Is that your child?" I asked. "One of

them, señorita. I have twelve." And he vaguely
indicated the rear apartments of the flat. He liked
silence, and he got it, from twelve children in a
Madrid apartment!

During that summer of 1934 agrarian trouble,
always and naturally rife in Spain, was very much in
the news. In June there had been a widespread
peasants' strike, and in Catalonia a fiercer tussle
was on over Companys' *Ley de Cultivos*, which
legislated for the establishment of arbitration
courts to settle disputes between proprietors and
lease-holding cultivators of land in Catalonia. The
terms of such arbitration were to be favourable to
the depressed and long-suffering cultivators, and
the landlords having opposed it and the tribunal
of appeal having flung it out, Companys defiantly,
but strengthened by the support of the people,
ratified the law. All through the summer there
was excitement and anxiety over the situation thus
created, and lengthy speeches on the matter filled
the papers. And in early September the Catalonian
landowners held a great meeting in Madrid to
protest against the application of the *Ley de
Cultivos*. And Madrid came out on lightning
transport strike to protest against the landowners.
This was the trumpet-call of a State of Alarm, as
they call it, throughout Spain, which was to attain

its climax, on October 5th, with a general strike all over the Peninsula and the proclamation of martial law in Asturias.

But from a balcony in the Puerta and to the non-prophetic eyes of a foreigner, this beginning of battle and tragedy did not seem what it was, and because the *madrileños* are so appreciative of their own crises it had, in fact, a welcome entertainment value.

A party of the Catalonian landowners—some in fancy regional costume—lunched in my hotel, to the disgust of the old goblin waiter, who was socialistic. He made faces behind their backs, and was very slack in serving them. He imitated their Catalan speech derisively to me, but my linguistic talent was defeated, alas, by this flight of mockery.

The Puerta, with everything at a standstill, was considerably livelier than on normal days. Crowds of amused men, women and children flowed about it all day in extreme good humour. Every time a *guardia civil* cautiously started off a stray yellow tram there was delighted applause; every time anyone entered or left the shabby Home Office on the south side, he was amiably insulted and cheered. Lorries full of armed *guardia de asalto*, moving slowly through the crowds, had flowers, kisses and wine-skins thrown at them as if they were

popular matadors. And, efficient and severe
though they look, they are popular. They are of
the Republic, and have as yet no tradition of
ruthlessness behind them.

Madrid likes nothing better than an excuse to
stroll and stand about and pick up news. A
transport strike offers perfect conditions for this
pastime, so perfect that, although the weather was
intensely hot, many people seemed to forget the
need of a siesta. For the sake of hanging round and
missing none of the comedy of the strike, they
even bore periodic searchings for arms by the
police with the greatest amiability and interest.
And sometimes when their crowding became too
thick or if a youth shouted something rather too
rude about the government, an exasperated
guardia, firing a shot in the air, and shaking his rifle
at peaceful spectators in balconies, would get a
round of applause vigorous enough to satisfy
Belmonte on his luckiest day. Indeed, no un-
informed looker-on could possibly have guessed
that that merrily-conducted protest strike was,
and was by the *madrileños* understood to be, a
significant warning of anger and despair. The only
touch of the latter which one noticed on the
Puerta during those two days was the sad shrug
with which stroller after stroller, crossing over to

the gates of the public lavatories, discovered them
to be locked.

Some Spaniard—I have forgotten who—has said
of Madrid that it contains everything necessary to
human happiness, viz., cafés, the Prado Museum
and three bullrings.

It is certainly a good centre for bullfights—for if
on any Thursday, Sunday or feast-day of the season
none of its bullrings offers an attractive *corrida*,
which is unlikely, there is sure to be one at
Toledo, or at Aranjuez, or at least a *novillada* at
Alcala de Henares. But the more usual difficulty
for the *aficionado* is to choose between seeing
Lalanda fight at Guadalajara or El Soldado in
Madrid's new ring at Ventas.

I first saw Belmonte fight in Madrid. It was a
specially grand *corrida* to celebrate I've forgotten
which feast-day. The *espadas* were Belmonte,
Lalanda, Ortega (since killed in civil war), and
Manoel Bienvenida. A very famous quartette, and
the prices of the seats were high. Tickets were
much coveted, but mine—not a very good one,
about the tenth row of the *tendido* in the shade—
had been secured a full fortnight in advance.
Traffic in Ventas promised to be dangerous and
difficult that afternoon and as no one is ever late for
the *corrida*, and as it always starts on the stroke of

the scheduled hour, one shortened the siesta considerably although the day was torrid, and set out in good time for the bullring.

I was in my seat at a quarter-past four—with fifteen minutes to spare. People poured in on all sides. The immense place was going to be packed as perhaps never before. Excitement and good humour seethed. It was a perfect *corrida* afternoon —no breeze, brilliant sunlight, no movement in the blue sky.

As the hands of the clock moved on towards half-past four, as the President arrived, as one noticed the *quadrillas* assembling behind the high gate in the *barrera*, it seemed to me that the rows of seats among which my own was situated were becoming unnaturally crowded, with a great many people standing up among them and talking rapidly. Attendants looked worried and asked us to sit closer together, *por favor*. Soon they were asking the impossible, and people still stood arguing in front of all the occupied seats. *Guardia de asalto* looked on gravely, and shook their heads. A man directly behind me was speaking with such speed and passion, apparently to someone a considerable distance from him, that it was impossible for my foreign ears to get his drift. The talk and crowding were becoming almost

unbearable when, just as the *alguaciles* came out to
start the ceremonial of the great *corrida*—the truth
dawned simultaneously on everyone concerned.
A block of about 250 *tendido* seats, of which mine
was one, had been sold twice over, in error.

Well—Belmonte was taking the first bull, but
alas, for five hundred of his devoted fans he might
as well have been doing so in Mexico City. We
were all on our feet in a flock, five hundred lawful
claimants to two hundred and fifty seats. The
outbreak of astonishment and condemnation was
majestic as a tidal wave, and made Belmonte, whom
we were all obliterating from each other's sight,
seem temporarily unimportant. We were con-
ducting, by one accord, a protest meeting of the
most harmonious and unanimous kind. We were
at one. There was no quarrelling and no stampeding. We had all been fooled—my neighbour, my
neighbour's wife and I. Five hundred of us
shocked into passionate disapproval of folly.
Every voice was raised, but none against the man to
left or right; all, all torrentially and most
castilianly against 'las autoridades, la empresa.'
Nobody pushed or kicked, but nobody could
possibly sit down and somewhat clear the view
of the arena until he had said as fully as
possible all that was in his mind about this piece of

carelessness. The police and attendants understood this necessity, and made no attempt to force things out of the natural. They stood by in sympathetic silence. The man behind me was an orator of the kind that needs something to strike with his fist, and something to wave in the air. My shoulder and béret answered his two requirements. Every now and then the young man on my right generously broke up his own speech to protest to the older man on behalf of *la señorita extranjera*—the foreign lady. His protests were always received with complete courtesy and agreement, my shoulder remorsefully patted, the béret replaced with Chanelesque solicitude. But eloquence is intoxication. The next second I was thumped again, and my béret whirled above my head. *"Qué burros, qué tontos que son esta empresa! Jesús y María, es una burla más grande!"*

Thus, in the fifteen minutes allotted to the killing of the first bull the tidal wave rose and fell with—granted the disaster—complete satisfaction to everyone, no tempers lost against the innocent, no scapegoats victimised, and certainly no bones broken. By the time Belmonte was taking the round of the ring with the enemy's ear in his hand —according to Monday's papers he killed that bull very characteristically—the whole five hundred of us were quite calm and had discovered that we could fit in somehow in the space of two hundred and fifty. So, while still taking a grave view of the situation, we decided to sit down and observe Lalanda.

The English are reported to be exceptionally good-tempered and jocose *en masse*, so I suppose— I've never been to a Cup Final—that such a situation as the above would somehow have been turned into a joke by them and their benevolent bobbies; in Ireland or Wales I'm certain someone would have started a row, and I think that in France the affair would have turned to pandemonium. What would have happened in Germany? Here in Madrid it was by no means a joke, but neither was it a rational being's excuse for blacking his brother's eye. Castilians, excited, tend to know exactly what they are excited about and are single-tracked and therefore almost calm in expression of excitement. Perhaps it is their sober habit of life which gives them this accuracy and decorum in emotion, this ability to keep their eye on the ball. It is an attractive gift, and I thought this occasion a good demonstration of it.

I am not disposed to talk of bullfights here. They are a controversial subject, as I know who have madly been led into quarrels over them. In any case, as I can never find a defence of them to placate my own conscience, how am I to defend them to others more sensitive? I believe it to be impossible for anyone of northern blood to sit through a *corrida* with an easy conscience, or without moments of acute embarrassment and distress. Nevertheless, the thrill and the beauty can seduce; more than that, can be remembered with longing. For the *corrida*, much more cruel than fox-hunting—if cruelty can be measured—is, unlike that pastime, a great art, a symbolical and most moving spectacle of which the unavoidable cruelty is no more than a necessary incidental. Bravery, grace and self-control; the cunning of cape and sword against incalculable force; sunlight and the hovering of death; comedies and tragedies of character; tinny music timing an old and tricky ritual; crazy courage and sickening failure and the serenity of great matadors curving in peril along the monstrous horn. There is no defence. Either it gets you, or you're sick.

I have seen it get, or almost get, the most unlikely people. Stephen, for instance, Ruth's mother. (I mentioned Ruth in an early chapter, also in connection with the bullfight.) Stephen said, as everyone says, that she thought she ought to see one. I was very doubtful about that. For though she is sane and a realist and no doubt could visualise in advance the worst that she might see, nevertheless she is extremely tender-hearted and protective in her attitude to cats, birds, children, and all defenceless life. Also she had recently been very ill.

However, she attended a *corrida*. That afternoon the unfortunate horses suffered badly. The picadors were cowards and the bulls very brave. There were some terrible moments, and seeing the ashen colour of Stephen's face, I wanted to leave after the second bull, and after the fourth. But she preferred to see it through. At the end she was unhappy and profoundly exhausted, but she admitted, reluctantly indeed, that she saw seductive beauty in the ring and an inexplicable nobility. "But I don't want to see another," she said—and looking at her exhausted face one felt that that was best. Still, lately I have heard her recant. Safe in England with no immediate danger of invitation, I have heard her say that, in fact, she would like to attend another *corrida*.

Two men, friends of mine who without having seen a bullfight quarrelled bitterly with me because I insisted on its beauty, at last went to see one—largely out of friendship for me, I think, and to give me a fair hearing, as it were. For some time afterwards they were silent about their reactions, until at last I found courage to ask them point-blank for their verdict. They had been shocked indeed, but not, as they had expected, to the exclusion of every other emotion. With considerable alarm they had felt fascination too. One of them, however, declares that he could never in any circumstances attend another. The second feels that he would be unable to resist seeing it again. Yet these two are absolutely matched, I should guess, in that English sensitiveness to the feelings of animals which, I freely confess, runs more thinly in me, a mere Irishwoman.

I have sat next to an American millionaire and millionairess at their first *corrida* and watched him carried right out of himself by the new experience, eager and puzzled, but anxious to understand it, anxious to see another, baffled and made young by an irresistible emotion, while she, massaged and smooth in her foulard, visibly didn't give a damn for the thing one way or another, unconcerned alike for horses' wounds and matador's genius, contented because she was working her way through another bit of the European programme— as undisturbed as her neatly waved hair. I have seen an elderly Englishman struggle with his need to be sick while his undergraduate companion cheered Armillita's *banderilla* work until he was hoarse, and was dragged protesting from the ring by his green-faced companion. I have sat in *barrera* seats next to a Frenchman and his wife who had only that summer discovered the bullfight and were pursuing it all over Spain—he, because he loved it and she, in Eve's tradition, because she loved him. This was their fifteenth in four weeks, and in *barrera*, or front-row, seats—that Frenchman told me. And she, who held the spectacle in horror and was terrified of it, sat at each one of them with her eyes tight shut while the bull was in the ring, but courteously, so that Spaniards should not be offended, concealing her voluntary blindness behind smoked glasses. "But why attend them?" I asked. "Because he likes my company, and I like his." And so, through all the *corridas* of that summer, I suppose, they sat in the front row, she with lids down behind her dark glasses, he holding her hand and roaring his pleasure at the brave *toreros*.

Then there is Mary, the painter. At her first bull-fight—she being one of the English animal-fans—she took an outspoken loathing to the entire Spanish nation. Became so abusive indeed and so disposed to hiss that I had good reason to fear an international brawl, and begged her to leave the ring with me. But no—she would not do that. She would see the thing through and give it what she called a fair trial. She continued to behave very obstreperously, however, taking exception to the applause which those around her saw fit to concede the fighters. Again I begged her that we might go home rather than stay to insult the Spaniards, who after all had not compelled us to attend their bullfight. No. She could not make up her mind to leave. "Though, what do they think they're clapping, the asses?" I was growing peevish. "Try to find out," I said.

La Serna came out to take the third bull. A middle-aged white-faced man without theatrical appeal. He encountered a very fractious bull, inclined to keep *querencia*, that is, take up a fixed, defensive position, awkwardly close to the *barrera*. It looked like being a difficult and messy fight, and my heart sank. For Mary's mixed and vigorous reactions were in train to become embarrassing. It was obvious that, morally, she was panic-stricken, but that the stimulation she was deriving from the brilliant and garish *mise-en-scène* was a shock and surprise which she could not resist. For though this was a rather shabby and provincial bullfight, the day was glorious, the *quadrillas* were brave and graceful and the bulls impressive enemies. It was in fact a good average *corrida* for a foreigner to see—by no means a show occasion, but alike in its defects and merits representative. And that it was taking the painter's eye and emotions I did not dare suggest to the raging, over-wrought moralist beside me. She was going through a storm and I could only sit still and hope that whichever side of her won we would get through without 'an incident'—which seemed unlikely.

However, La Serna fought his difficult bull. Not spectacularly. There was no scope for flourish against so immobile an enemy. But with patience and courtesy. With perfect fairness and with the grace of self-command in every gesture. And at a moment which seemed completely impossible he profiled, went over the horn and administered death as resolutely as if he himself was made of steel. His performance was an excellent pre-sentation of tragedy—which always ends by tranquillising the witness. Certainly it quieted Mary, and, I think, brought the scales down for her on the amoral, or immoral side. Not that her struggle is ended—any more than it is for other *aficionados*—but rage though she does again and again at the ringside, and suffer though she may, she pursues the *corrida*, and is a committed "fan."

Often since that day in moments of anxiety in the arena I have heard her—good Catholic that she is—half-audibly offer God the most tremendous pledges will He only save the *torero* then in danger. But whether or not, her prayer being heard, she keeps her fantastic promises, is of course between her and Heaven.

Madrid's second contribution to human happiness is a good effort. The Prado Museum. *The Times* shows us photographs nowadays of its stripped and desolate galleries, and we look at them with relief, thankful that the treasures are at present safe from Franco and his allies. That they should have been saved from destruction while children playing nearby in the Calle Atocha had to die is admittedly a bitter gratification, but two wrongs never make a right, and in our tragic day we must take comfort where we can. Though indeed the world could probably proceed tranquilly enough without all the Murillos and Riberas of the long gallery, whereas the parents of those babies are unlikely to do very well hereafter, remembering their manner of death. But *à la guerre comme à la guerre.*

When will the day come when Goya and Rubens take their ancient places that we may stroll before them again placidly arguing, superiorly smiling at the judgments of strollers fore and aft, and dodging the low-murmured ecstasies of patriotic custodians? Dodging above all the old chap in charge of the Goya drawings upstairs. For he is to be feared as the Ancient Mariner. In a room containing about four hundred drawings—the 'Tauromaquia' among them—he is liable to hold you viciously gripped for half a minute in front of each, while he explains it. For the average sight-seer that is a somewhat long time. In any case it is too long to be held by the elbow. He is a formidable old man, a man with a mania.

Downstairs on the main floor one is freer. Taking a great number of bores for granted and since a tourist's time is limited and gallery-crawling the most fatiguing of all pleasures, necessarily ignoring, too, a host of excellent painters, though not Coello, whose modest half-dozen are beautiful and arresting—the people who can most profitably be examined in the gallery are Velasquez, El Greco and Goya; Nicholas Poussin, Tintoretto and Titian; Paul Veronese, if you like him; and Peter Paul Rubens, overwhelming in his glory.

Rubens lived in Spain for a year in his early twenties and again for a year in maturity, when he met Velasquez. Also all his life he enjoyed the patronage of the governors of the Spanish Netherlands, was used by them on his second visit to Madrid as a diplomatic envoy, and in Antwerp as well as in Spain executed many commissions for the Spanish King. And it was in Madrid that he first saw, copied and was influenced by the work of Titian. So that it is not surprising that the Spanish national collection boasts about seventy of his works.

It is often said authoritatively that he was greatest as a religious painter and that his 'Descent from the Cross' in Antwerp Cathedral is his best canvas. This I am unable to understand. I do not think that he was a religious painter at all in inspiration, but an executant of immense efficiency and extrovert quickness, who, living in a time of religious tranquillity when princes and cardinals were building churches again, was supremely able to deliver whatever was required in the way of a picture. His baroque and pagan gusto, so much of his period, seems much more the real truth about him. And here in the Prado—nymphs, Graces, Venuses, Dianas, Mercuries; myths, allegories and radiant worldly portraits—we have it all flung out as if to sweep away the walls behind it, as vigorous, complicated and nobly springing in execution as it must have been innocent and uncomplicated in origin. Pure painting. Seizing on any old myth that caught the lively, happy sensibility, and painting it gloriously out of sheer excess of ability and life. Without weariness or hesitation—and the bigger the canvas the better for him, he said. He was indeed a giant at his work, and his exuberance seems to us now as vast and remote a legend as any that he painted.

And when we turn away from him to Goya, we turn from the pure painter *in excelsis* to someone very different—historian, satirist, novelist, journalist, matador, patient, bitter individualist, angry spectator of his own day who happened to be mainly a painter. Spanish history from 1780 to 1830 can be learnt from Goya in the Prado, and his great feeling for life and for Spain may be measured in the immense range of passion, mockery, nightmare and beauty which his work encompasses. If it is disconcerting to remember that the man who painted 'Dos de Mayo' and the 'Desastres de la Guerra' did in fact for a time side with Joseph Bonaparte against his own people, an explanation may be found in the moody and tempestuous individualism of the Spaniard, or in the court painter's loathing—recorded for ever in his portraits—of Charles IV and his dreadful wife, Maria Luisa. In any case his work is an overwhelming retribution, and Spain forgave him long before he died—in Bordeaux in 1828. Nearly a hundred years later his bones were brought back to Madrid and now lie in the Church of San Antonio, whose walls he decorated. The Casa de Campo and the meadows of the Manzanares, where he liked to watch and paint contemporary life, and where he would now find more disasters of another war, lie very near without, and the enchanting worldly angels which he painted for San Antonio keep frivolous guard over him. His models for them were young society beauties with all of whom he is said to have slept, and he has generously demonstrated on these walls that each possessed in full her five earthly senses and a disarming dash of original sin. Thus he is suitably sepulchred, and even the gigantic memorial head of him outside his temple, though very absurd on its stumpy pedestal, cannot really insult him. An American lady said in my hearing that it is "as vast as his spirit." But it's vaster than that, and if Franco's bombers don't hit it, that will be a minor disaster of the war.

After Goya, Velasquez, so grave and intelligent, is perhaps *en masse* somewhat boring, just as El Greco is a shade fatiguing. I have heard the latter called the first romantic in paint, but is it, in fact, romanticism to reduce all subject-matter to a frantic and rigid formula? is not romanticism essentially liberal in feeling, and the source of naturalism? Velasquez's landscapes, richer and sadder than Corot's, have a sentiment and fluidity dangerous and literary, if you like, but romantically evocative as the mediæval and dogmatic ecstasies of El Greco never are. Agony and asceticism are always personally formalisable and are eternal, but individualistically, though El Greco has handled them, it yet does not seem as if 'romantic' is their index word. To narrow and enfever—if you like, to infect—inspiration, however individualistically, is not necessarily to romanticise it, and El Greco, lonely, strange creature, seems to me, if classifiable at all, much more related to the formal mediævalists and primitives than to the romantic movement. He is said to have been homosexual, but that suggestion can be of little use to us in considering his work. More mighty than he have been touched with that peculiarity, but the residue of all emotional experience tends in spirits large enough to be at last of natural and universal value, whatever the personal accidents of its accretion.

However, to discuss El Greco without taking the brief journey from Madrid to Toledo is very foolish —and to Toledo I am not at present in humour to return. For one thing, the recent battle of the Alcazar sticks in my heart and makes me angry. Such bitter waste of courage! Such an insult to the spirit of history! Spaniards holding a Moorish fortress against Spaniards for the advancing, returning Moor. For anyone who has loved the long history of Castile—unbearable. There is only one comfort in it—that the Alcazar, dominant though it was in the city's fantastic skyline, is of all Toledo's ancient architecture the specimen least to be regretted. It was, in fact, like all Alcazars that I have seen, a dull and heavy piece of fancy-work.

The Moor indeed laid his fanciful hand a bit too much on Toledo for my taste. Frilled gates, turrets, horseshoe arches, *mudéjar* ceilings, filigree and fretwork—these things infuriate me, flung higgledy-piggledy against Castilian good sense and seemliness. So, not even for the sake of seeing the 'Burial of Count Orgaz' again—El Greco's greatest picture, and perhaps one of the greatest in the world—not even to walk again through the pure Gothic naves of the Cathedral, or to sit in El Greco's garden, or to see where Calle de La Trinidad embraces Calle Carlos Marx, or to hear the bells of a hundred convents string the night with prayers; not even for the sake of leave-taking, of looking back at the evening-lighted roofs so magically and eternally assembled on their golden hill, not even for supper in Aranjuez—asparagus and strawberries in a garden-restaurant of that murmurous and shadowy little town—for nothing, in my present mood, will I return to Toledo. It has magic, and can enchant—unless the heart, as perhaps mine was, is out of tune. So if I remember Toledo more as a teasing legend than a town that pleased and wooed me—I must blame only myself, and perhaps somewhat the Moors.

There is another town near Madrid—Alcala de Henares, where Catherine of Aragon and Cervantes were born, where Cardinal Cisnero de Ximenez founded in the fifteenth century a university which almost from its beginnings rivalled ancient Salamanca in scholarship, where the first Polyglot Bible was edited, and where they confect a delicious kind of sugared almond. I would be glad to spend another feast-day in Alcala. Indeed, I'd be glad to live there for a while. It is a long, straggling, ribboned-out kind of place, rather Flemish-seeming, flat on the plain. Streets become grassy roads there, and then suddenly are squares. Almost all its façades are lovely; all are crumbly and unself-conscious. In summer it is very dusty, very pale. The music of its trees is brittle-sounding. There are pink-and-white villas, with

EL GRECO'S GARDEN, TOLEDO

tall iron gates and heavy guelder-bushes. Gipsies
hug its outskirts, sleeping all day among rustling
grasses. Under its portals on market-day any kind
of commerce may be effected. There are good,
unpretentious bull-fights often in its unpretentious bullring. The beer is cold and strong.
There is an illuminated bandstand. And if you
don't like it, there is a little railway station, and
Madrid within an hour.

I liked it, and would like it again, would like it
any time—well-bred, ancient, untidy, gracious
town. But eastward is not my route now. I am
bound north. The trains that leave Madrid from
Atocha station are not setting out for me. I must go
north across the capital now. I have not praised it
half enough. I have told nothing of its sibilant
acacias, its garden cafés, friendly bootblacks, pretty
children; of its gay, courageous, ancient slums; its
elegancies, its clubs, its flying witticisms. I have
said nothing of the theatres and cinemas that begin
their last programmes at eleven p.m., of re-
staurants where one may sit and talk till dawn, of
how natural it is to stroll in the Paseo de Prado at
four a.m. and take a homeward tram at five; I have
said nothing of the Plaza Mayor, of the National
Palace, of University City, of the Retiro—or of the
night clubs on the Paseo de Rosales, the 'dancings'

on the Florida; or of listening to flamenco-singing, far away and late, from the Toledo bridge. I have not mentioned Madrid's amazing sky, or the view to be had on every side of empty, blond, austere Castile. I have not spoken of the gaiety and graciousness that make the town lovable from end to end. Because all such memories bring sorrow now, a sense of love that is unbearable. Madrid besieged by Spaniards, Madrid disfigured and tormented—is always, so great is her heart, most recognisably Madrid, but no one who has ever loved her can linger now too much upon her lighter, happier graces. The thing to note is how these have, by latent character, become transmuted into heroic and eternal decoration. *No pasarán.* The enemy of all that is individualistic, free and libertarian cannot subdue the least posturing of Castilian cities. Madrid may wear a flippant, cosmopolitan face, but it is the capital of Spain and is unperturbed by that responsibility. *No pasarán.*

SERMON IN KITCHEN SALT

AT the mention of El Escorial all guide-book writers and almost all travel journalists start to groan. "Cette énigme de pierre," they begin at once, and "cette façade monotone et froide." Says Gautier—"le plus ennuyeux et le plus maussade monument que puissent rêver . . . un moine morose et un tyran soupçonneux." Says Barrès—" . . . le paysage de l'Escorial, tourmenté par de sombres passions . . ." "Without freedom neither beauty nor truth is possible," says Justi, generalising bravely. "The spirit of stern etiquette which Philip impressed on the Spanish court . . . looks at us with petrifying effect from his building." And "impressing beholders with a conviction of its indestructibility . . . it seems to stand with sullen determination . . ." says Mrs. Pitt Byrne.

All of this could be dismissed in one of several short words which the printer would not print.

The generations have been telling each other that
Philip II of Spain was a cold, unattractive and
sinister riddle, and that he built this palace-
monastery-tomb on the Guadarrama for unattractive and sinister reasons of megalomania,
morbidity and fanaticism. They don't know this
by the book, but they have taken it in with their
mother's milk, as it were; they know it through
the lazy common ear which delights to absorb
platitudinous legends. A sinister, desolate notion
from beginning to end, that monastery of Saint
Laurence, and telling each other so as they drive
out from Madrid the tourists shiver superstitiously
and by the time they reach the sunny upland
where the great building rests in peace they have
become so wrapt in history, as they think, that
they do not see what is spread before them, but
only what they came out primed to see—the
dreadful *chef-d'œuvre* of an unpleasant man, the
expression in granite of a tormented and cold
spirit. So they begin—"le plus ennuyeux et le plus
maussade . . ."

Philip remains unanalysed, unexplained, the
historians tell us. But he has lain corrupted a long
time now, in this Pantheon which he raised for the
Spanish kings, and whatever his dreadful motives in
building a monastic retreat—one of them was to

fulfil a promise made to Saint Laurence, should he hear his prayer for aid in battle and give him victory; and can any descendant of the long Christian story find morbidity in that?—whatever his hysterical motives, the stones raised at so much cost and with so many over-anxious dreams, having taken the sun and rains of more than three hundred years, wear now a very quiet, unalarming and unvulgar look of austerity and peace.

No one, looking at Versailles, thinks: "How dreadful, how insane, how morbid as a monument to self!" We may find it pathetic, or vulgar, or wicked, but it does not strike the average tourist as a pathological expression—oddly enough. But because Philip II was Castilianly in love with death, not with life or with himself, and because he expressed that love with an extravagance of restraint, we shudder. And yet, though in the ABC of æsthetics he did not succeed in externalising his idea as excitingly as his strutting little great-grandson manipulated his, on the whole he went one better. He had the more difficult thing to say, but actually in some ways the more durable and sane, the less psycho-analysable.

Although his elements were strongly mixed in Philip they were, in fact, too mixed and not quite strongly enough. Remarkable, even formidable in about six or seven important ways, he was not finally, personally, eternally remarkable in any one way. So compensatorily, as we say nowadays, his proud necessity found two escapes from this disappointing realisation. Extrovertly, as man of action in the world, he projected himself as exponent of God's Will, Heaven's First Secretary, sword and voice and splendour of the Eternal Church against Germanism, heresy and England. And introvertly, as would-be poet and weary sinner, pathetic contemporary of Saint John of the Cross, he turned away from life, which failed him, to the alarming, unpredictable drama of death. Not with the pure desire of Saint John of the Cross who, shamelessly in love with God, saw the last agony only as a gate to perfection, threshold to the ineffable embrace, and cared not a snap for it in itself. Not like his other great contemporary, Saint Teresa, whose cry of desire was *"Muero porque no muero."* (I cannot translate this line without crippling it. I have tried many times. Word by word it means, "I die because I don't die.") Philip was not, like these others, a poet, nor as an earthly lover does he seem ever to have been able to love in such terms as these two mystics would have understood. He was always rigidly and pitifully trapped within himself, and thus in his flight towards the vision of death we find him still stiff and unrelaxed, still failing of the blessedness of self-loss, and establishing only a terrible self-dramatisation with which to placate his perpetually sore and uneasy self-esteem. Thus in the first place, death, the death of a king of Spain, is for him an occasion of pomp so intricate and endless that a lifetime of organisation and attention to detail is necessary to do it justice. Humanity, which notoriously enjoys funerals, must be merciful here to this exaggeration in Philip of a trait that is existent to some extent in most of us. When we die we do the most certain and common thing of all, the one thing that no one ever doubted we should do—but, curiously, in being so platitudinous we acquire always a brief strangeness. For a day or two between death and burial, we are as if original or remarkable in some way to those who stand around and order flowers. Joining, as our grandfathers loved to say, the great majority, one paradoxically becomes almost unique for a little while. And our most natural and unavoidable situation is made, by a universal human whimsicality, our most—perhaps our only—dramatic hour. Many a man's funeral is the most picturesque and lively event of his life, could he but be there to see it. Philip understood this with a touch of madness, and vicariously, as it were, he took much elaborate pleasure from his own demise —as indeed from the demises he planned with liberality for all his descendants in perpetuity. So sitting in the Escorial palace, mostly in pain and disappointment as he aged, mostly weary, troubled and overworked, he planned the Pantheon and the Church, and the elaborate network of ritual and etiquette with which Spain was to lay him to rest and pray for his soul. The arrangements and instructions are quite shocking to read; the worked-out splendours are terrible. The whole scheme is the expression of a nature tragically determined to be outrageously important, or know the reason why. And beyond the funereal pomp, beyond the laying away in porphyry and marble of the weary, disappointed but so important carcase of the King of Spain there was another, less assessable preoccupation. What of the soul that would have fled from it in that important hour of death? If Philip could but have loved a little the God he served with such desperate meticulousness! Indeed, we feel always as we pity him, if he could but have loved any living being, how great he might have been instead of pathetic! But here, in his foresight for his soul it is as usual all foresight, all anxiety—and taken to the plane of madness.

The mystics of his day and race, Saint John, Saint
Teresa, Fray Luis de León, and the painter El
Greco whom he encouraged and sought timorously
and unsuccessfully to appreciate, all these in their
different terms were in love with what they saw
beyond human life, but Philip, who prayed
incessantly, who slept in a room so ordered that
his face was for ever turned to the High Altar of his
church, who sought God determinedly and re-
pented his sins in wearisome reiteration, Philip
saw beyond his own funeral not the blessed
surrender of his petty self to a transcendent eternal
goodness which must do as it willed with one
sinner and at the last be utterly trusted—but only a
tough and violent drama, a crazy struggle between
hosts of devils and angels for the eternal possession
of his so important immortal soul. Compensatory
self-inflation with a vengeance. He saw eternity by
no means as release from self, but as the phantas-
magoric setting for a demonic war about that self.
It never occurred to him that the true blessing of
death might be the end of self-importance; that in
any case would never have seemed a blessing. He
was trapped. He was a gigantic Malvolio. And so
he laid his plans for the battle that might wage for
ever about the disposition of his soul. And these
plans—the instructions, the burden of prayer for

him which he laid in perpetuity on the back of the unfortunate Church Militant—well, as an example of pathological megalomania it would be extremely terrifying did not the arid impotence of such madness render it merely sad. ✕

All this is true of him. El Greco painted his dream—that the cosmos might be for ever in conflict over whether he was a saint or a sinner. It makes Protestants shudder. But Catholics, wishing Philip the eternal rest he could not allow his pride to believe in, can only smile, I think. One lonely egoist's manipulation of the doctrine of sin and damnation to placate and inflate a private psychological disease does not explode a theology— and few Catholics are afraid of death. Philip was neurotic—and it is necessary to mention his neurosis here because something of it has certainly been expressed in the tombs and in the religious regulations and etiquette of the Escorial.

But he was neurotic perhaps only to the north-west. For he was a many-sided man, and a man of outward self-control. He could accomplish much and have many excellent practical ideas, control an Empire, direct communities, study liturgical niceties, read philosophers, fuss over his children's health, be an attentive husband, plot vengeance and butchery, build an Armada, pursue a lust, reward and cherish faithful servants, snub the Vatican, argue with architects, give alms to beggars and lay out orchards, while manipulating always on the side his dream of death and judgment. And the Escorial is no mere fruit of his neurosis, but a memorial to his versatility, and the remnant of a great attempt at full, collective life.

For really his idea was a good one. The village, farmlands, monastery, palace, hospital, school, library, church and gardens of El Escorial were to be a serious experiment in communal harmony. Everything which is necessary to the full life of the good, the honest, the wise, the intellectual, the ascetic, the skilled or the creative was to be available there. All the arts and crafts of living were to be cultivated with liberality. Experts in building, engineering and agriculture were invited from all over Europe to partake in the scheme. Medicine, horticulture, forestry, music, the sciences and the philosophies were pursued there. The school professors had to be men of real quality, and intellectuals from anywhere in the world were welcome to pursue their researches and to make full use of the great library on which its founder lavished money and thought. The principle underlying the whole thing was dictatorial. The monastery, under Philip's sharp control, owned miles of land about El Escorial, but this and its population were now to be managed and developed for their own good and brought to as high a degree as possible of general comfort and culture. The dictatorship was benevolent, and founded of course on a questionable system of charity. But Philip's charity was true and constructive, and reading his directions for the conduct, for instance, of the hospital which was at everyone's disposition, one cannot but be struck by the man's sensitiveness and his so non-contemporary sense of human decency.

But El Escorial was to be something more than a collectivist experiment and a gesture towards progress. Philip was the Sword of the Church, and this ambitious settlement was to be an answer to Lutheranism, which accused Catholicism of ignorance and the encouragement of ignorance. A taunt which was completely intolerable to this active-minded believer. Learning must flourish here in the generous soil of faith, and German mockers must be silenced. Also here—and in this the would-be artist in him had his head—here no trouble would be spared to reassert at its fullest the Church's ancient æsthetic splendour against which all the heretical thunders rolled. Here, while northern Europe fumed, Heaven would have, at

EL ESCORIAL

Philip's command, its full traditional glorification from the arts.

Above all, however far its possibilities might stretch, El Escorial was to be, Philip said, an unswerving activation of the Council of Trent. It was to stand for that, and to make clear to all the centuries that human life could be best, most justly and most fruitfully conducted under the thumb of that famous codification.

He grew old and ill and he died still working passionately at his beloved scheme, which was to succeed somewhat in this and that, but in general fail. But he did not see or admit that. And given his time, his code, his strange nature, and his terrible capacity for crime and mad pride—it seems to me difficult not to feel touched and attracted rather than repelled by his Escorial. As a ruler he did some frightful, and some noble and disinterested things; as a young man he appears to have been a cold and unsatisfied sensualist, with, pathetically enough, a great and generous ad-miration for the splendidly free sensuality of Titian; as a friend he was grateful and true; as an injured or suspicious friend implacable; as a husband he seems to have won the affection of his four wives; as a father he was anxious, kindly and even playful. He certainly was a man of parts—but the Escorial is associated mainly with the best of him, and his sanity and kindliness are represented by it, and his active desire to be useful. So are his self-reproaches and disappointments, and his pathetic search for normal peace. (He loved to fish in the rivers of the neighbourhood, and was a good fisherman.) So are his escapism and his terrible fantasy-life, his mania for death.

It is, in fact, an interesting building. Not 'ennuyeux,' not 'indestructible,' and not, I think, 'un énigme de pierre.' Your first sight of it, if you drive out from Madrid, is impressive and even formidable. You will have been bored, and probably very hot, for most of the journey. There are stretches of Castile, and a certain area north of Madrid is one of them, which are just scrubby, stony wastes with little to recommend them— least of all the smart, ultra-modern villas which a few commuters have inexplicably erected for themselves in the dusty and undistinguished plain. But eventually, climbing noisily, you will rediscover verdure and pasture, and native, rural life at its most grave and lonely. You will rediscover the immensities and variations of the *llanura*. And then, having passed near to a famous *corral*, *ganadería*, or farm of bull-fight bulls—which may or may not interest you—you will see above you,

beautifully placed against wooded hills, the towers
of Philip's monastery. In the sunshine, pale grey
and severely lined, they look magnificent. But
when you have descended from your bus in the
upper village, when you've had a drink and seen
how leafily and contentedly the little town sleeps
against the northern side of the great monastery,
you'll be in a better state for dealing with your
impressions.

Gautier described Guadarrama granite neatly
when he said it was like kitchen salt. It feels very
like that against the hand and it glitters. This
glitter makes the whole place look paler and
lighter in sunshine than it, in fact, is. In shadow or
rain all the stone of this place is mouse-grey. The
street straggles under noble trees up to a pleasing
little square with simple cafés and where steps
smothered in tangled flowers lead to another hilly
street, with arcaded shops. There are hotels for
tourists, two of them very good, and one of these
two with an enchanting wilderness garden. There's
a very odd little cinema, there are places where
one may dance. In summer there is much
animación, for Philip's mountain resort has a
brilliantly lovely summer climate, and is admirably
suited for all kinds of outdoor pursuits. So when
Madrid grows too hot, many *madrileños* come up

here to the hotels or to holiday chalets. And the village itself is quite populous and comfortable. So when the tourist passes between the pleasant, solid granite houses which Philip built for the palace staff, and takes his first close-up view of the stone enigma, he may be surprised to find its long open northern and western courts simply swarming with children, nannies and courting couples. This rather knocks the 'atmosphere' out of the 'gloomy pile,' but the long and noble façade really loses nothing by it. The courts are immense and are separated from the road only by slung chains, and on the west side by a low flat parapet which makes a splendid seat. The monastery walls fling stretches of agreeable shadow, and there is ample space for rounders, love-making, knitting and breviary-reading. The Spanish mania for the *paseo*, that sociable, frivolous, indeterminate and adventuring stroll, is amply provided for in the courts of the Escorial, as well as in the clipped shrubby garden which runs along its southern side, and whence there is an incomparable view, over ponds, orchards and cornlands to the white Gredos and almost to the Sierra de Toledo. This garden simply riots in children on sunny evenings, and the noise there can be sometimes terrific; but the black-robed monks pacing in twos or alone in

the galleried cloister above do not seem disturbed
by it. It is a garden full of lovely smells, and sitting
there in a cool hour, hearing bells ring and motor-
horns sound a little way off in the village, half-
stunned by the children's riotous, ante-bedtime
hysteria, watching monks and farm-boys at work in
the fields below, and the cows and goats assemble
at the farm gate for their milking—one gets something of the human conviviality of Philip's idea,
and marvels again at Gautier's "le plus ennuyeux et
le plus maussade . . ."

Doric severity was somewhat overdone in the
architectural design, undoubtedly. Such graces as
ravish on the façades of the Plateresque hospitals of
Santiago and Toledo might have done no harm to
El Escorial. And bigger and fewer windows would
have made for a more endearing nobility. But that
said, there is really little fault to find with such
perfect proportioning, such inspired relation of a
structure to its setting and its function. Within it
is again architecturally noble, but disappointing
both in its lack of decoration and, for the most part,
in such decoration as it does possess. Philip was
unlucky in his fresco-painters, and much too
cautious about sculpture and all forms of orna-
mental relief, and his great nude church, which is as
a structure entirely magnificent, cries out for (*a*)

the removal of such ornament as it has been given, and (*b*) that *carte blanche* be allowed some genius to bring all its essential nobility to life. Here in this church over which he slaved one feels very strongly the power and the pitiful limitations of Philip's judgment. And here too one remembers an amusing story. The Archbishop of Toledo was in the sanctuary, proceeding with the confirmation of certain of the royal children and with them, as Philip always insisted in such things, of any children of the village or surrounding farms who were prepared to receive the sacrament. The occasion was one of immense splendour and ritualistic pomp, as Philip adored such occasions to be. The choir performed with a perfection which outdid Rome itself; all the brilliance of the Spanish hierarchy was in the canonical stalls; Philip, his family and the Court were in their stalls. Incense, flowers, candles, silence—and the Archbishop proceeded to confirm the children. But one little peasant boy had apparently not been told what to expect when this sacrament was administered to him, and when the Archbishop, great prince of the Church, gave him the ritualistic slap on the cheek—perhaps he overdid it—the little boy, true Spaniard of the Spaniards—sprang to his feet and shouted at the prelate—"You son of a bitch!"

All things taken into account, that made a good situation, and the Court and the priests knelt paralysed. (No one seems to know what the Archbishop did.) But Philip II, most pompous of ritualists and dévotes, burst out laughing. And the ceremony went on without further disturbance.

As you descend under the church to the Pantheon of the Kings you will, willy-nilly, fall in with other tourists from your native land—because you can only go down there at stated times and in large batches. If this happens, listen or not as you please to their comments on all that the guide is telling them of the ceremonies of the Spanish Court in its great days. But if you do listen—when for instance they are told that no king might lie in the Pantheon until five years after death, and must spend those five years in a chamber half-way down, the *pudridero* or room of corruption—I wonder if you will marvel as I have so often done at the English reaction of amused incomprehension to foreign ritualism and pageantry. The English have, in their formal life, a devotion to mummery and ancientry that is simply unbeatable anywhere. They have Black Rod and White Rod and all those uneasy-looking Clubmen who, on the proclamation of a king, as we have lately seen with unlooked-for repetition, get themselves up in tabards and read quaint sentences aloud at various points about the town. They have Gold Stick in Waiting, and the Yeomen of the Guard, and the changing of the Guard, and the Trooping of the Colour; they have 'Pop'; they have the Freemasons; they have the Knights of the Garter and the Knights of the Bath; they have Toc H, and they have Two Minutes' Silence. They have the Royal Courts, the Royal Enclosure and the Royal Yacht Squadron. They are jealously devoted to all these ritualistic mysteries, and no one grudges them to them. Indeed, all these things are very interesting and attractive to many foreigners. And always when an occasion for public ceremony approaches, *The Times* takes off the file that serviceable old leading article we all know and like so well, which begins: "We English have a genius for pageantry . . ." Doubtless you have. For my own taste, English pageantry is a shade too beef-eaterish, too brass-bandish, too well-drilled. But that is neither here nor there. The English have—*The Times* having said it many more than three times it simply must be true—a genius for pageantry. They have also had in their time a genius for conquering the earth and that might have taught the whole breed, one would think, how to be detached and polite before the varying foibles of the races. But curiously, in observation abroad and above all in Spain, I have found that in any group of tourists, French, German, American, etc., listening to a guide, only an English voice finds it necessary to express facetiousness against 'old, unhappy, far-off things.' It is a form of nervousness, no doubt—but it is odd in an imperial race. And one day in the Pantheon of the Kings—which is ugly, cold, ornate but not at all funny—an Englishwoman and her boy friend were so much moved to honest mirth by the whole thing—the *pudridero*, the shelves of coffins, the empty coffin waiting for Alfonso XIII who now will not be allowed to occupy it—that the guide and the rest of us, not English, were very much embarrassed. But the two Britons didn't notice that. In the Sacristy they nearly 'passed out' over El Greco's Apostles. I don't know, indeed, if they got home from Spain without rupturing themselves, they found everything so funny. When, in Philip's simple, whitewashed study, they were shown the stool on which he rested his gouty foot, that practically finished them. They got together in hysterics over the 'bad old lad.' They were very disconcerting to the guide. But they didn't seem to find El Escorial 'ennuyeux.'

Neither perhaps did the unpleasant, stupid prince who became Charles IV of Spain and whom

Goya painted so magnificently and terribly. His indulgent father, Charles III, built him a little country house here at El Escorial, in 1770. It is down the hill from the monastery, in Lower Escorial, and it is certainly down the hill from Philip II's ideal of austerity. It is very Louis XV, very smart, very Boucher. It is a pity that the prince who was to enjoy it was not a more decorative and seductive figure, but no doubt the fun went fast and far there when he and his friends came out to hunt in the Guadarramas. It is an amusing eighteenth-century tag to Philip's quiet palace. It is filled with tapestries, consoles and period bibelots, and a great deal of Madrid's 'biscuit' china from the Retiro factory—tiresome and Wedgwoody—but the guide will be very much hurt if you don't rave over it. There is, however, something melancholy, and thus attractive, about the little empty museum-house with its secretive air of old naughtiness, old nastiness, and its slender windows looking out on a wild, aromatic tangle of neglected garden and dark wood. One wonders somewhat pruriently what did, in fact, go on in this remote, expensive little pleasure-house.

Sleep a night or two in Escorial, if you can, tourist. Even if the monastery is not so very much your cup of tea. Even if the summer gaiety and graciousness of the village tires you, and perhaps offends your obstinate conception of what is due to the sinister Philip. For the sake of standing on your balcony, late, late in the night—and it will have to be late, for holidaying Spaniards won't leave the cafés and the cool, leafy streets until about three a.m. at soonest—but stand on your balcony then, if it looks southward or eastward towards Madrid, and gather up as much as you can for memory of the Castilian night. There will be a lamp still burning on the street corner below you, and the blue-white road will be stained with moving shadows of the trees. You will not see the monastery but will perhaps a little feel its peaceful presence away to the right beyond the trees. Ahead of you, the ground will slope away, roofs and a few lights slanting rapidly down the hill to the lower village. Someone is almost certain to be singing—boringly correct, as that may seem. Someone is always singing in the night in Spain. Useless to deny it. The *llanura*, the great plain of Castile, will be before you, 'all Danaë to the stars.' Infinitely suggestive, deep and subtle. Most noble and patient. No sign of the white Gredos now, but they are there at the edge of the blue darkness. And blue it is, inky-blue, not black in its deepest places, that calm, embracing sky, its few stars as exaggeratedly bright and liquid as if each one was Sirius. And the air—the aromatic, flowery air! Try to keep that night in full remembrance, tourist. I wish I could.

BLONDES AND FOUNTAINS

GETTING from El Escorial to Segovia by train—it ought to be quite easy by bus and I have forgotten why I didn't go that way—is a small-size version of getting from Santander to Burgos. You have to describe a very wasteful triangle, and kill a great deal of time at the apex—a railway junction called Villalba, one of those startlingly desolate railway junctions in which Spain abounds. Dumped there from a slow afternoon train you stroll out of the station to see the sights, and in five minutes, unless you are a passionate sociologist and wildly interested in every facet of the life of your fellow-men, you have seen all you can stand of them. For a more depressing social nucleus then Villalba it would be difficult to find. A few verminous old houses of red clay; a few more of new red brick; a road surface that has somehow established itself without one hand's turn from humanity; a broken-down

motor-van; something that looks like a dead
gasworks. A rubbish dump with a dog asleep in it.
The village idiot, a cripple girl, a baby with ring-
worm, the other village idiot. As I say, if you
carry a heart and not a blue book in your breast
you return in five minutes to Villalba station.
Your brothers, humanity, live whole lives in lost
places like this. But what can you do about it, dear
fairy godmother? And anyhow, if someone tried
to run a café that might cheer things up. It would
at least cheer up tourists.

But there is a café in the station, you find—and
its tables are urbanely set out on the very long
platform. You sit down and order beer and it is as
cold and lovely here and the glass is as frosty as in
the Alcala in Madrid. And as you drink—and
smoke, to the politely expressed amusement of the
old commercial traveller from Logroño who sits at
the next table, and who is very pleased to study the
habits of *las extranjeras*, the foreign ladies—as you
drink, the evening grows cool and turns towards
Spain's *paseito* hour—and here too in Villalba.
For suddenly, from God knows where, from inside
the dead gasworks perhaps, an entire gay populace
is on the platform, and strolling up and down, up
and down. And the station turns out to be
Villalba's *alameda* or boulevard. All the café tables

are filled and soon walking has to be very slow indeed. But that is how Spaniards like it. The sociable crowd overflows to the other platforms, and soon groups are calling to each other and dashing to and fro in great friendliness over the railway lines. Trains come and go meantime and there is a good deal of uproar—we are on the Madrid–Bilbao main line—but no one gets killed. The waiter tells us that the station is always like this—Ah yes, very animated—in the evening.

There are girls, linked together as usual in fives and sixes, in their usual shiny make-up and with their hair carefully waved and fixed against their heads. Very neat, as usual, and moving easily and gaily—full of pleasure in themselves. But to my mind shrill and disappointing as their lovely, distinguished country never is. Out for their usual bit of evening fun, they are pleased to find the novelty of two foreign females on their boulevard, and for a particular reason some of them pass and repass our chairs with what begins to be embarrassing frequency.

Garbo and Jean Harlow have in the last six years or so set the women of Spain quite mad on the 'blonde' question—and no race of women that I know of takes these matters of beauty culture with such unfortunate seriousness as does the Spanish.

There are Spanish blondes, but actually they are rare birds, and very lovely. Some years ago their brown- and black-haired sisters thought nothing much of them, but now they are envied and studied with passion. A genuinely fair head has become for feminine Spain the only symbol of glamour, and in the sincerest form of flattery astounding and sad things are done to less fortunately coloured locks. In country places and in provincial towns now, where the local chemist's advice has been taken or where instructions from the woman's page have been incorrectly—or correctly—followed, one sees sad and fantastic crowns of glory. Striped heads, black and gold like a football shirt; platinum surfaces with solid mid-brown underneath; olive-green *coiffures*; middle-aged pates of iron-grey sporting honey-coloured haloes. As Spanish women never wear hats, these simple efforts may be appraised without difficulty by the curious.

Well, on that summer evening in Villalba, feminine interest and enthusiasm received the stimulus of the century. Mary, the painter, happens to be fair in the Swedish sense, possesses an intensely fair head of hair. And the girls of Villalba, struggling hard to be polite, did not know how to contain their amazed admiration.

The possessor of this mythical trophy, this golden fleece, having as usual got herself mixed up in goings-on with various beggar-boys, did not at first notice the sensation she was causing, but I did and I knew why. We had had milder versions of this astonishment elsewhere in the Peninsula. I dislike as much as anyone else being involved in a public commotion. I smiled ingratiatingly, almost apologetically at the girls, who were now beginning to mass themselves somewhat about our table, holding up the *paseito* for less astonished citizens. But my smiles were not even seen, let alone returned. All eyes were on Mary's hair. I mentioned the situation to her, and when she turned towards her 'fans' I could see how they ached to lean over and feel the hair, pull at it, see if it was a wig. But they did nothing like that. "*La rubia*," they murmured dreamily, "*la rubia*." The blonde!

I paid for the drinks, and suggested that we might walk along the platform, and as it was getting dark now perhaps lose her admirers in the crowd. We got up—but we would have done better to stay where we were. There was a deft rush for the best positions close to the *rubia* and so off we set, surrounded, mobbed. Up the platform, down the platform. Girls simply swarming on us, smiling, gentle, but implacably fascinated by that head of hair. I must say I've seldom felt a greater fool in my life, and I've seldom disliked an inoffensive crowd of people as much as I did those sweeties of Villalba. But I don't honestly think the *rubia* minded very much.

After hours and hours of it—and sheer, delighted pandemonium it became as we tried to calm them down with tags of conversation—the train came in. And how the porter fought his way to us with our bags through that mob I've never understood, or how we climbed on to the train. Our departure was a triumph—all the girls yelling '*adiós*' and the *rubia* waving back at them, like a film star leaving Waterloo.

Well, that's Villalba. An unexpected place and we gave it a thrill. But I prefer Segovia.

Perhaps to enter it at dead of night is as good a way as any other. You don't see much, it is true, as you jolt from the station in the hotel bus, although the proud hotel porter is making you look this way and that exhaustingly and vainly all the time. But then he says in a *very* proud tone: "Look, there it is, just ahead—quick!" And there it is, and you drive under it, and it's behind you and it's gone, and you've had an impression you'll never lose, and never convey, of Trajan's Aqueduct. Ghostly, hardly visible, seeming darker than the dark sky. Still carrying the water of the Riofrío on the top of its ninety-foot arches. Still doing its job, full of power and beauty. Alarming somehow to a tired traveller at dead of night—seen even for a mere three seconds.

A great thing about Spain—for the traveller—is the Spanish liking for late hours. Arrive at any provincial hotel of the simpler kind—I cannot answer for the grand, international places—and you will be welcomed as if it were noonday. Not fussily at all, but then at no hour of the day will a Spaniard willingly make a fuss. But merely with quiet acceptance of the fact that here you are and that naturally all you require before retiring is the mere trifle of a six-course meal. It's an attitude that has its points.

Supper was heavenly, and heavy, that first night in Segovia, and served ceremoniously in a corner of a large dining-room already marshalled for the attack of to-morrow's dustpans and brooms. All the chairs were on the tables; all the épergnes and tantaluses were draped. It was an amusing feast; we spoke in whispers, but ate and drank a long time, to the contentment of the waiter.

I love Spanish hotels. I speak, I repeat, only for the cheap ones, of which I know a great many now. They have their defects, Heaven knows—

occasionally quite unpleasant defects of a kind
which we need not discuss in this polite book.
Defects of plumbing. But these are infrequent, and
their like has come my way in the hotels of other
countries where I have been charged more than I
have ever paid in Spain and where compensatory
efforts of hospitality were neither as marked nor as
much to my taste as the Spaniards'. Good manners,
for instance. Spanish good manners are un-
beatably good, and most of the Spanish possess
them. They are so especial because of the steady
balance in the average Spanish character of good-will
and reserve. These two things are ideal in a hotel-
keeper—as in anyone. And good taste. The good
taste of Spain when she isn't trying is only equalled,
in my experience, by her bad taste when she is.
And the latter can certainly be frightening. And
as we are talking of hotels—you may be received,
say in Valladolid or Zaragoza, into a lobby where
the proprietress has made every effort to please
your capricious eye. It will be terrible, very likely.
There'll be statuary that you'll never forget as long
as you live, and a radio as big as a bathing-hut;
there'll be oil-paintings of Sevillan ladies, and
flashier strip-lighting than you've ever seen—and
the proprietress, pleased that you want to stay in
her smart place that she has tried so hard to make

attractive for you, will lead you to your bedroom, over which, assuming that you only want to sleep there, she has not taken quite so much trouble. And it will be a big whitewashed room with two long, balconied windows. If the house is an old *palacio*, the floor will be of white or black marble, but it may be only of wood, scrubbed white. There will either be an immense old carved wooden bed with a faded blue coverlet on it, or a low, wide, modern single bed—this the more likely—with narrow simple head and foot rails. But whichever it is, you'll be astonished at the excellence and modern comfort of the mattress, and almost embarrassed by the liberality with which you will be given clean sheets. There'll be running water—and sometimes it will even be hot in the hot tap—in any Spanish hotel where you pay ten or more pesetas a day for your full keep. (Ten pesetas is not quite six shillings.) There'll be a light by your bed. There'll be a mirror, perhaps one that makes you look funny, on the wall. There'll be a little round table. There'll be a wicker chair and another chair. There may be an enchanting old wardrobe. There will certainly be a bent-wood hatstand, circular and very tall, of the kind that one sees in offices over here and in Express dairies. And it is probable that the whitewasher, before he gave up, expressed himself by running a thin gold line or two, or perhaps a pale blue line broken by occasional true lovers' knots, along that level of the wall where in happier climes people put a frieze or a picture-rail. In fact, it will be a dream of a good, sweet bedroom, so long as the *señora* was not ambitious to make it *muy moderno*. And in the hot siesta hour when the shutters are drawn, as you lie and consider that whitewasher's gold lines or his blue—so wavy, so individualistic, so exactly all that the room needed to give it a place in memory—as you observe how the shadowed whiteness and bareness is blue here and buff there, and yellowish where the sun falls frequently—as you enjoy your room, in fact, you will realise why Spanish women, on the whole, are not beautiful—because they try so damn hard. Let them alone, let them grow up and grow old away from cosmetic shops and movies and women's pages, away in their lost mountains—and they are beautiful. I have seen them. But give them the *moderno* notion, like the hotel proprietress, and, for some reason of simplicity or I don't know what, they are done. It's an odd thing, and a pity. Because why should they not be modern? Who wants a world of 'hey nonny nonny'? Still, there it is. Spain's native taste, grave, common-sense, individual, is lovely, but that particular kind of cosmopolitan taste which she is snatching at now is terrible—the worst there is around. However, perhaps internationalism is not all to blame. The Moor long ago imperilled Spanish judgment with his arty-and-craftiness. Imperilled and infected, but mercifully did not dominate. Still, his legacy remains a menace, and I, for my part, detest all signs of the Moor in Spain.

Alfonso El Sabio ('El Sabio' means 'The Wise') did not. He was the king of the eleventh century who plays such a heroic part in the *cantar de gesta* which celebrates The Cid. Although a great Christian king—he brought the Cistercians to Spain, established the use of the Roman instead of the Mozarabic missal, and hammered the Moor on many a hard field—he was susceptible to the influence of Arab art and learning, and even openly took a Moorish princess for his mistress. (He appears to have been a great womaniser.) He was so much impressed by the Moorish fortress or Alcazar at Toledo that he built another such at Segovia, on the high western end of the great rock on which the town stands. His structure is no longer there, but another built in the fourteenth century, and practically burnt away and restored in the nineteenth, stands on its site. I have no taste for Alcazars, though they are usually well placed, as is this of Segovia. It is like the great prow of a ship, which is the town. It contains a museum of firearms. If it contains anything else, the firearms dulled my mind so much that I retain no other impression. But there is a room in which, says the guide, Alfonso The Wise one day thought out for himself very courageously that the earth moves round the sun. However, just as he reached this heretical conclusion he was warned by a horrible flash of lightning to give over—which he did. And in repentance founded the Society of the Cordon of Saint Francis.

There is also, I seem to remember, an ugly Moorish throne on which Isabella the Catholic and her husband Ferdinand were wont to sit. But that is not really very interesting. What *is* interesting is the noonday view west and south from the parapet of the Alcazar. But by now my readers will have tired—though I have not—of the plain of Castile. Seen from this point, however, a slight novelty is introduced. The guide points out to each batch of tourists that, from a certain corner of the parapet, the outline of mountains resembles the naked, recumbent figure of a woman—news which instantly restores the weariest party's interest. His claim is examined with thoroughness and the

184

sightseers descend from the parapet seeming more jovial than when they went up. A large nude, undoubtedly.

It is curiously difficult to describe Segovia from memory. It has an untidiness and variation of aspect that cannot well be assembled into one impression. Avila is easier to see whole in retrospect, so is Santiago. But this spread-out country town which exists mainly as a market for the wheat, wool and hides of its province, and which is generally filled with countrymen in their sober, attractive regional dress, does not come back to me with the same unity. Westward, near the buff Alcazar and its pleasant green square, my memory is of very white houses and little white churches, of brilliant green trees and flowering bushes. Down in the centre of the town the big square is dark-grey of face and even in torrid sunshine uninviting. Its cafés are fly-blown, its bandstand excessively productive of music. The one cinema seems a ridiculous place outside which crowds are always stampeding against doors that never open. The centre of Segovia has somehow a dirty, unhopeful and obstinately backward atmosphere, although nearby on the Salón de Isabella II—quaint name for a little city park, but one which that rakish queen might have smiled at—one finds flocks of sophisticated and exaggeratedly well-cared-for children playing with very modern toys and supervised by impressive nannies. Here one gets back an impression of light and floweriness, and here the view again is wonderful. And above, behind, the Cathedral rises—buff-coloured and noble. Modelled on Salamanca, but more successful in result, certainly more beautiful inside, and with very beautiful cloisters, in one corner of which, madly exposed to all weather an enchanting fourteenth-century picture, painted on wood, illustrates the story of Maria del Salto (Maria of the Leap) who sleeps in the tomb below it.

Maria was a Jewess, and married. Let us say that she was a beautiful Jewess. One day she was taken in adultery, and her husband, being a man of the very highest morality, decided that the thing to do was to throw her from the top of a high rock on the outskirts of Segovia. According to the picture the whole town came out to see him do this. And he did it—the action hurting him, no doubt, more than it hurt her. But Our Lady intervened. She caught Maria in mid-air for all to see, and bore her in her arms and in safety to the ground. The beautiful Jewess lived many years to enjoy the kudos of this miracle. She became a Christian, of course, and was buried with honour in the

Cathedral cloister. But it is amazing that it does not occur to anyone to take the picture of her great adventure indoors out of the damp.

There is a little church in Segovia which was once a synagogue and has a Moorish ceiling and many Moorish shapes and signs in its architecture. It is an odd experience to go to Benediction service there. One felt half afraid all the time. It seemed as if some supernatural disaster must attend so odd a marriage of ritual and setting. But none did on the evening I was there, unless one might describe a very boring sermon as a supernatural disaster.

Downhill southward from the Plaza busy little streets of shops where the countrymen buy their supplies run past the romanesque and lovely church of San Martin, to the open square at the edge of the town across which the Aqueduct strides at its greatest height of ninety feet and whence its whole visible span of one hundred and nineteen arches goes swinging east across the valley. At any hour, in any light, it is a spectacle of heroic order. In its thorough utilitarianism and efficiency completely Roman. Practical indomitability alone gave it its beauty. It was necessary to raise the conduit to the height of the Segovian rock. So the natives and the imperial soldiery, flogged and bullied to it, no doubt, heaved out the blocks of granite to their exactly required shapes and piled them on each other in this long double line of carefully graded arches. Without mortar or clamps. It is a beautiful piece of work. Blue sky and straggling landscape smile from the east through its succession of lofty frames; farm-carts and buses pass underneath with Lilliputian indifference; dogs and gipsies take their siesta in its narrow shade; and in the niche above its tallest arch where the triumphant builders suitably placed a statue of Hercules Our Lady stands to-day —no doubt somewhat surprised at her position. It has withstood all the battles, sieges and commotions of Segovia's history and still, austere and glorious, brings the Guadarrama waters to the city, as Rome ordained.

And underneath its noblest arch, just below Our Lady, you take the autobus for La Granja. This is a summer palace of the kings of Spain, situated about seven miles from Segovia, on the slopes of wooded hills above the village of San Ildefonso. It was built in 1719 by Philip V, the first Spanish Bourbon, who was homesick for Versailles. A curious focus for nostalgia to take in him, one may reflect, for he was a man of severe and prudish temperament, a pupil of Fénelon and a critic of contemporary frivolity. Yet he built this little palace as a pleasure dome where he might be at peace and remember France.

Patriotic Spain waxes hot over his success—but, in truth, he did not succeed very well. La Granja has charm, but mainly of the accidental and natural order, and enhanced now by that melancholy and dreaminess which settle on forsaken pleasaunces. But it assuredly is not a second Versailles. The palace is architecturally attractive and well-mannered, the more so for being quite small—not a palace at all, in fact, but the stately house of a man of taste and moderation. The gardens, however, exist mainly as a setting for a series of twenty-six ambitiously conceived and fantastic baroque fountains which, on the whole, at least when out of play, strike one as facetious, coy and too many. They play only on certain feast-days —I have never seen them do it—and all Madrid joins the exuberant autobus rush from the surrounding provinces to witness their sparkling splendour, and have a glorious picnic. In the sunshine against the background of dark woods their music and sparkling mist and the gay faces and voices of the holiday-makers must indeed make up the characteristic kind of Spanish pleasure-scene that Goya loved so well—and Diana and her Nymphs, twenty of them, in a very big fountain group at the

end of the long avenue, and pretty enough in
weekday stillness, must come to very lovely life
when all their bronze limbs are drenched and
shining and the waters cloud and sparkle about
their heads. But one feels a crowding of frivolity—
too many and ingenious are these waterworks
pressed together about so sober and simple a house
—the idea of them does not seem to fit with
Philip's character, or his idea of coming here, even
though Versailles had fountains too. So that one is
not surprised to read in the guide-book that they
were all added to his original scheme by his wife
while he was away on a long journey, and that he
said on his return, looking gloomily at Diana's
Bath: "It cost me three millions and amused me
three minutes." It might a little placate the rather
worried and scrupulous mind of the king if he
could know how nowadays the whole Spanish
populace adores his fountains and also nothing
better than to make them an excuse for a day out.

Hills, very dark with trees, rise east and south
beyond the gardens and beyond the artificial lake
that feeds the fountains, and make with the Castilian sky an impressive horizon appealing to a
meditative or nostalgic eye; and the water-garden
which drips down from this lake through a series
of mournful and unfacetious fountains, to end under

the terrace and windows of the palace, must surely have given Fénelon's moralising pupil a gentlemanly satisfaction which he sought in vain in his wife's expensive toys. Certainly that stretch from the house to the lake is good gardening, and worthy of France. And the whole park, which belongs to the people now, is a pleasant place to loaf in on a summer evening, offering room and allure as it does alike to those of Philip's temperament or of his wife's. And as La Granja, like El Escorial, has an exquisite summer climate, it is a holiday place well loved by *madrileños*, and has in its season, like Philip II's rural seat, a mild and umbrageous gaiety about it. It is peaceful certainly, and solitude must be always in its gift—but not now, so far as I could see, the solitude which Borrow reports of it, so great that "wild boars from the neighbouring forests . . . frequently find their way into the streets and squares and whet their tusks against the pillars of the porticoes." I did not see that happen in the village of San Ildefonso. But no reader of Borrow needs to be told by any other writer of the military rising against Queen Christina in this palace or of its repercussions in the Puerta del Sol in Madrid. How magnificently he tells that exciting story! La Granja, built as a refuge from Spain by a lonely Frenchman, the Spanish king, had all the same, like that unwilling monarch, to take its share in Spanish troubles, for here Godoy, the lover of Maria Luisa, Charles IV's unattractive wife, handed Spain over to France in 1796, and here, too, most of those manœuvrings and jugglings with the succession went on which brought the Carlist wars and all their troublesome repercussions on the nineteenth century. Spanish history has a way of seeming to lie heavy about the tourist in every Spanish village that he enters—and here, too, by all means in La Granja. But sitting under the trees of the Paseo del Palacio to drink, looking downward at the tall, untidy village, and admiringly at the lovely old white houses that curve up in a slow arc on either side to meet the palace gates— one is reminded, in fact, of France. Some pleasure village in the mountains near Grenoble, the name of which escapes? Or is this place a little like Montreuil? Did the first Spanish Bourbon succeed somewhat in forcing his desire?

But the bus is sounding an impatient horn. It is time to go back to Segovia where Trajan, the Roman Spaniard, gave such a noble start and signpost to Spanish history.

MAINLY PERSONAL

IT seems as if the guide-book writers and I can never agree. One which lies open in front of me now says of Burgos: *"Son site est nu et sévère; son climat est très chaud en été, très froid le reste de l'année."* Surprising! Admittedly I do not know Burgos well. I have passed through its landscape more than once, but have only stayed in the town for one short visit of two days. But they were summer days—and mild and rainy. Even somewhat cold. Indeed, as far as climate went, Burgos might have been Canterbury or Winchester. Nor did the locality seem *"nu et sévère."* It is in my memory a leafy town, grey and green, and with its full, flowing river scuffled by wind. It stands nearly a thousand feet above sea-level, true enough, on the edge of Old Castile, and just south of the great Cantabrian mountain range. The plain all about is austere, not lush; but it is rivered, fruitful and patiently farmed, and it has always seemed to me that a traveller approaching Burgos in daylight and seeing from the train its quiet grey masses, lacy moving trees and two slim spires arising from amid them undramatically, must get an impression of deprecatory unimpassioned peace not often suggested by a Spanish town. And this impression stays, though modified by closer acquaintance with the busy, natural liveliness of the streets, and their provincial hustle. For it is a cathedral town almost in the English sense.

Legend and history weigh it to the ground, naturally. For this is an ancient capital of Castile, and was founded as such by Alfonso III in the ninth century—since when up to date it has never stayed very long out of Spain's front page. The Cid—El Cid Campeador—is its greatest son; Wellington, who beat the French out of it in 1813, is probably the greatest foreign soldier that ever trod its streets. But no doubt there are many glittering alien generals strutting about there nowadays, making themselves busy on Franco's side against Franco's fellow-countrymen.

Spain has two, even three Cids. There is the Cid of history, soldier of fortune, lively and brave, always playing his own hand and fighting Christian or Moor exactly as immediate policy directed, until he made himself king of Valencia and Murcia.

There is the Cid of the "Cantar" and all the ballads arising from it—an epic Cid, a flower of chivalry, a type of knightly valour, a very considerable bore. And there is, according to one determined school, the Cid who did not exist at all, but is merely a composite of many gallant and greedy Castilians of the eleventh century. But be these three as they may, if one had never heard of him before, in twenty-four hours in Burgos one will have accumulated quite enough data about the hero to satisfy a mild curiosity. His trunk is in the Cathedral, his bones are in the Town Hall, the testament of his betrothal to Jiména Diaz is among the city archives, his statue is in every other niche about the streets, and his name is on the lips of any tout who spots a foreigner. In short, one must love Spain very much indeed not to grow somewhat weary of El Campeador when visiting his home-town.

Indeed, to be just not only to the Cid but to the general glories of Burgos, to investigate them as they deserve, one needs to be in vigorous and widely receptive mood, and perhaps one should arrive there at the beginning rather than at the end of a sightseeing tour. In any case two days is not enough. The effect of Burgos on one who has only two days to spend there is liable to be almost paralytic. One sinks into a café chair and throws up the sponge. Or that at least is what this one did—more or less.

I was tired in Burgos. Disappointed too. I had counted on a bull-fight, and there was none. But the cafés are good. Big and civilised, and mostly ranged along the Paseo del Espolón which fronts the river—so that as you sit and shirk, most of the glories you should be examining are completely hidden behind your back. And the parade of modern Burgos is agreeable to watch. The middle classes are out on the stroll, according to custom; they seem prosperous and inoffensively pleased with themselves, the young men producing their usual cumulative effect of dignity and near-beauty, the young women not quite so idiotically coiffured and made up as in other towns. A band plays under the trees; as you sit you buy shares in lottery tickets, and beautiful long ties to take home to gentlemen friends. The weather is too cool for iced beer, so you drink manzanilla or coffee. You have your shoes cleaned. Nothing so agreeable when you are tired as the soft, polite gossip of the Spanish shoe-black who paints your white shoes with meticulous care, admiring them as he does so, but astonished and pleased to know that you prefer the shoes they make in his country. You grow sybaritic in your café chair. Burgos' past is behind you—and what of it? You make no guess at all, in your lazy blindness, at its so near future. Beyond the theatre at the end of the Espolón are the Cavalry Barracks; and spurred officers, strolling about, give the final thrill to the girls *paseito*. In spite of all the modern comforts and amenities about, the pleasant, bourgeois scene is very old-fashioned really, quite nineteenth century in its invulnerable pleasantness, you think. Burgos—so soon again, and so unfortunately, to be a pivotal point in Spanish history— seems in August, 1935, a rather more gay and friendly cathedral town than most—a cathedral town with a garrison.

But it is no good. The cathedral is on your conscience. You paid good money and took some trouble to get here to see it, and you can sit in a café anywhere. Ah, *turismo*, what a slave-driver you are!

So you leave the Espolón and pass under the Arco de Santa Maria. Under it. You don't go in, though, as it is the provincial museum, no doubt you should. But you don't like it much externally. It was built in the sixteenth century in honour of Charles V, and it is turrety and fake-seeming. Besides, according to the guide-book, it contains only some tombs, a few *mudéjar* doorways and *"parmi les tableaux, d'une valeur médiocre . . . une tête de Christ par un*

peintre inconnu (les larmes sont d'une réalité saisissante)."
We know those *"larmes d'une réalité saisissante."*
Spanish churches and museums drip with them.

You find the cathedral just beyond the Arco—
and, if you are a really serious tourist, your work
is now cut out. You must walk round it first—all
round. That is easy. The flagged squares are
empty, except for children playing *pelota*, and slum
houses, rising like cliffs beyond, are remote and
indifferent. The ornate, vast church is, in fact,
quite lonely and at your disposition.

It was begun in the early thirteenth century, and
was worked on for three hundred years. And if
immensely decorated Gothic is what moves you
most in architecture, here in Burgos you have indeed come home. For my own part I am in two,
or three, minds about it. It is very fabulous; very
credulous and passionate. Lovely but only by an
effort comprehensible. Not like Romanesque,
which appeals at once to human ideals and intellectual human sympathy; not like Baroque, which,
good or bad, appeals to or arouses human sensuality, human vanity, human nature. Gothic ana-
lysed is obviously the work of men of flesh and
bone; it is indeed narrative and explanatory to an
exhausting degree, but in its best results it is mad,
impassioned and naïve to an extent which wearies,

if it does not frighten, the unlucky, dispirited adult of this century. The fault is ours. We are very far from the age of faith.

Useless to describe this church. More profitable to string together for our own pleasure what fragments remain from a staggering feast. A vague idea of the decorated glories of the façade and the octagonal dome, of the escutcheons and flourishes on the exterior of the Chapel of the Condestable; a clearer memory of great doorways and noble staircases approaching them, above all the stairway of the Coroneria. Within, riches crowding even such height and space. Gothic retablos, noble Renaissance tombs; the Condestable altar; the prettiest Santa Ana in the world; the fourteenth-century carvings in the chapel of Santa Catalina; a silver Our Lady holding her Child, sweetly jewelled and enamelled; a terrible Christ crucified, with a body made of some sort of soft leather, dyed to seem human flesh, and with human hair and eyelashes. And Papa Moscas (Papa Flies)—the usual toy, the great clock, in the form of the upper half of a gigantic funny old man who, swung above the nave, strikes a bell for the hours, and at each stroke opens his great mouth to catch flies.

That is all that I can remember—though the church teems. And almost all that I remember of

the treasures of Burgos. I did not go to see the
Carthusian house of Miraflores, about four miles
away; did not even cross the river to the snobbish,
thirteenth-century convent of Las Huelgas, or find
the house where Saint Teresa put up with so much
trouble in the last year of her life. I did not look
at the site of the Cid's palace. But I saw the outside
of another palace where Ferdinand and Isabella
received Columbus on his return from his second
voyage of discovery, and in which Philip the Handsome died. I remember, too, the arcaded Plaza
Mayor with Charles III in the middle, children
whizzing all about and attractive shops well lighted
under the arches. I remember good cinemas in
Burgos, good food, and a bedroom in which my bed
was lost in a daintily draped alcove of muslin. I
would have preferred less daintiness and to sleep
nearer the windows, but it was a memorable, large
room, and surprising because the lady of the house,
amiable but thickly warted, did not at all suggest
muslin to my mind. I lost Borrow somewhere in
the muslin—and departed towards the Cantabrians
—watched the two slim towers recede above a
summery cloud of leafage, admired at long range
the chapels, monasteries and palaces which, face to
face, had made me only lazy, and never thought at
all that snare and blunder lay so close in waiting

upon that happy-seeming cathedral town: I was impatient to cross the Ebro, to be in Vizcaya and in a town I love, where no real tourist ever goes—Bilbao.

Bilbao is the first Spanish town I ever knew. I lived and earned a living there for nearly a year when I was young and Alphonse XIII was still a merry monarch. (Actually Primo de Rivera pulled off his military *coup* and assumed dictatorship in that year—but I did not see that happen. I had just gone home.) It is a town of solid vulgarity and great melancholy. Although founded as a city in the early fourteenth century, it seems to have played little part in Spanish history until the nineteenth, and so is architecturally undramatic, unatmospheric. But the Carlist wars shook it to its roots and are not yet forgotten. In 1923 it was still natural for a citizen to tell you of his neighbour that he was a 'Carlista' or a 'Cristino.' And bourgeois families were still estranged and stiff with each other on that old issue which now must surely, in the nature of things, have blown away? However, in its time it was besieged three times by the 'Carlistas,' or upholders of conservatism, oppression and the divine right of kings—and three times proved unbeatable, so that Isabella I, silly and rakish queen, who had to be the symbol of the harassed liberals, called it the Invincible City. In the present war, the twentieth-century Carlists have more than once shaken their big fist at Bilbao, but different though this town is from Madrid in most things, like Madrid she will never be bullied. Steeped in local pride, in Basque nationalism, deeply and irrevocably Catholic and believing, Vizcaya is passionately democratic, passionately for justice and common sense. Franco's dream of non-representative, non-co-operative government of Spain will not mislead a humorous and reflective Basque. Bilbao may indeed have to face another siege—but she is used to winning them.

The river Nervión is navigable here for fourteen kilometres from its mouth, that is, right to the heart of the city. And as Bilbao, surrounded by great mountains, is the centre of very rich iron-mining and steel-founding industries, the port is busy and important. French, Belgian, English and German exploiters have had their lucky dip at this source of wealth, and their directors, engineers and imposing offices and banks swell the population and the ostentatious luxury of the new part of the town. (Though I suppose they've all been got away in warships now.) But the Spanish bour-geoisie has done very well for itself, by all appear-ances and has been more than a match for the helpful foreigners. The apartment houses of the left bank and the villa settlements of the sea-coast suburbs leave one in no doubt about that. Bilbao, by some ineradicable characteristic of landscape and sky, can never be caught looking dionysiac, or even merry. Her sober face is unrelenting, almost a judgment. But her luckier children have got used to that and plant their efforts at luxurious self-expression all about—incongruously enough, but without apology.

The mining villages nearby from which all this fatness comes are worth observation. Mining villages are admittedly of a pattern now all over the ridiculously mismanaged world. A pattern of vileness, not even of tragedy—for tragedy resolves itself into peace. I have walked through these villages, on pleasant afternoons of summer, and in winter too, through streaming mud. The one weather seemed of as little consequence as the other, as little use. The houses are always high, for it is a Spanish fashion to build tall and live apartment-life even in loneliest townships. They climb after each other, as a rule, these houses, along a steep gully of mud and stones which is the street. They are filthy, and almost empty of furniture. They have electric light and no other decency. In the dark wine-shop which is also the general store, there is almost nothing to be bought, but if you drink a glass of the local red wine, the harsh, good *chacolí*, and talk with the men about the doorway, you will hear little from them about life as it looks from where you and they stand. A shrug over the weather perhaps, a diffident inquiry as to your nationality, careful advice about your best road back to Bilbao. The reserved and kindly conversation of the Spanish bourgeois addressing a stranger.

These villages are awful in their stillness and despair. The crumbling Renaissance church, very filthy inside but recklessly *churrigueresco* of décor; the dilapidated girl at the brothel door; boys, pale and stooped, coming up the lane from their shift; a little way off heavily loaded trolleys rattling down the hill. And in the valley the pricking lights of Bilbao, outlines of banks and moving ships, softly sounding horns of Hispano-Suizas.

The bull-fights are good in Bilbao. I have seen great *corridas* there. I think that it was there I saw Mejias fight in 1934, on the Sunday before he got his last and fatal *cornada* in Coruña. Hemingway is very hard on Mejias, who had a long and successful career in the ring and who came back to it—wanting money, I suppose—at an age when so subtly timed an art must become intensely difficult. I only saw him fight on that one Sunday, his second last. He was grey-haired and thick-set, but a handsome, self-confident man, at ease with the applauding crowd and quite unafraid of the two terrific enemies he was asked to meet that afternoon. He showed off undoubtedly—but almost he had the right to. He took his bull kneeling. That is not particularly interesting to watch, but it amused the audience, and for a man no longer young or quick it was tricky. And later he passed him so close to the *barrera*, was so narrowly held between the *barrera* and the horn that the 'fans' cried out imploring him to forbear. A swaggerer perhaps, but gay and disarming that afternoon, when we were allowed to see nothing but courage and self-confidence. I liked him—*pace* Hemingway— and on the next Sunday night it was distressing to hear that he was dead.

The bulls are always very big in Bilbao. So is the bull-ring, almost as big as the new ring at Madrid. I'd guess. And round its painted parapet, behind the audience's heads, the names of all the great toreros of history are written up, reminding one of the writers' names in the British Museum Reading Room. One afternoon there I saw a young matador, fair-haired, pretty, greedy for fame, fight his dangerous bull with a display of graceful audacity which made me uncomfortable—as certain quite good-seeming actors sometimes make one feel. I could not assess his performance, which had an allure of brilliance. But the expert I was with said in sudden disgust: "This fellow's a vulgarian. He'll get the horn in a minute, and serve him right." And he did. He was carried out with blood streaming down his new pink silk. It was a bad *cornada*, but he recovered.

But why drag in this controversial bloodiness? Bilbao has other amusements than *corridas*. You can see the Basque *pelota* game played there at its best. There are two fine *frontónes*, or courts, and you pay very little to go in and can sit for hours watching long professional programmes. You can make bets on the players, too. The bookies stand in front of the graded seats and yell their odds all through the games. It is, as you know, a form of rackets, played in a very big court with a hard ball driven by *palas* or *cestas*, strapped to the players' wrists. The former are flat wooden bats, the latter wickerwork scoops, long and curved. The game, which is of the Pyrenees, is very much liked all over Spain now and in most towns of any size there are *frontónes* where professionals play every evening. Mary has seen girl professionals play it well, she says, in Sevilla. It is a very fast, exacting game. I do not see how girls could play it really well.

There are theatres—one big, ornate one

prominently placed by the Puente Isabella II—and
Madrid players sometimes turn up with a *zarzuela*
or a repertory of straight plays. There are con-
certs. I heard the Cossack choir sing there in a very
draughty concert hall. There is a municipal art
gallery in the slums, which is better than many
municipal art galleries. It has a few Velasquez; I
think, a Goya portrait, and, I know, a lovely Greco
"Annunciation." It has also a couple of acres of
Zuluaga. Zuluaga, a Basque, is the Sir John Lavery
of Spain. He is a bad painter, but his work is very
much admired. He lives in a Basque fishing village
called Zumaya, near Bilbao, and is very much liked
by those who know him. The legend is of a very
kindly, happy, locally patriotic and generous man.
He is a friend of bullfighters, and I believe that he
himself in youth entered the ring and tried his skill
against the bull.

The slums, the old town, are an area of high-
built, narrow streets. They swarm with crowded
life, the life of those who depend for it on the
dockside, and on the hells of smelting furnaces and
foundries which blaze unceasingly along each river
bank. There are noble, escutcheoned façades to be
discovered in this quarter, and some beauties of
ecclesiastical architecture—parts of the dark,
huddled, restored cathedral, for instance; its porch

and cloister—and the little battered church of the
two Saints John, and most beautiful of all, near the
art gallery, and near the market place, overhanging
the muddy, sad river, as implacably sober as the
town, San Antón. There are other churches, not in
the slums. There is the octagonal San Nicolás of
the eighteenth century; up in the new town where
is the ugly red Jesuit Residencia; also up there, but
nearer the river and in a quiet square of shivering
leaves and tall, sad houses, there is the soaring,
Renaissance porch of San Vicente. Very noble,
very melancholy, much enhanced by plane-trees all
about it. And up on a hill, up many steps, a
goodish walk, Santa Maria de Begoña. A miraculous Our Lady, dressed and bejewelled, with rings
on her fingers, in another ornate and satisfactory
Renaissance church, from outside which there is a
wide and complex view of all Bilbao, all its activi-
ties, successes and distresses, all that it might have
been and all that it is, its furnaces, slums, ships and
villas, its spires and bull-ring and winding river,
and beyond, its too rich hills and its debouch into
the Cantabrian sea, the Bay of Biscay. López de
Haro founded it well beside the mobile river and
between the breasts of hills.

Up here is perhaps a good place from which to
consider *le temps perdu*. I sometimes sat up here,

THE CHURCH OF SAN ANTÓN, BILBAO

on this same bench, twelve years ago. And this
return to Vizcaya is a purely personal pilgrimage—
for, as I have said, no one comes to Bilbao in
curiosity as a tourist, but some who have lived
there are curious to return.

I met a man lately who is now, like me, a
novelist, and who, like me, had a job in Bilbao in
the winter of 1922-23. We did not know each
other then, and I do not suppose that either of us
thought very clearly at that time of being novelists
later, though in that winter I began to attempt
dramatic writing. This man has said to me that
when he was in Bilbao he did not like it. "So much
mud," he said, "and that feeling of passions lying
close to the surface."

I have considered that, for the difference it shows
between us. I think we were both in our early
twenties then, but he, living a foreign life eagerly,
observantly and with generous interest—as he has
since proved in his work—understood intelligently
that he did not like it. I, on the other hand,
mooned along in a state of immaturity very much
behind my actual years, noticing little of any
importance, but cloudily and unintelligently under
the impression that I liked what I found about me.

The explanation of this difference is twofold, I
think. Firstly, there was my belated and lazy

immaturity of that time, which kept me much "in the moon," as we used to say when we were children, and which established an unfortunate and extended form of *esprit d'escalier* which I have not outgrown. I believe I never understand things until about ten years after they have happened. The present tense is rarely indicative to me. Secondly, he who did not like Bilbao's mud, and passions just under the skin, is English—and I am Irish. Mud was an ordinary matter in Ireland when I was young, and passions—so long as they be not sexual —are our familiars. So that the two things that fell new and raw on him were, I suppose, the two of all others which I took for granted and found home-like.

I remember the mud indeed. I remember the rain of that winter. I think I even wrote an article about it, which some unfortunate editor returned to me—unread, I trust. I also wrote a fancy piece about the Cantabrian mountains and Charlemagne's Roland—though what I thought Roland was doing so far west of Roncesvalles I can't imagine. I don't think I had the nerve to send that to any editor. But I know that I got the idea of it when crossing the Puente Isabella in torrential rain. So improbable is inspiration!

I was a considerable ass; very vague withal, and

unaware of my asininity. And I was often lonely and bored. But I see now, looking down from Begoña towards the bridge and the Arenal where I search for my own ghost, that I was pleased, in my roots, with the unexpected Spain I had found—and glad to an extent I would not realise for years to have opened up acquaintance with a country I was to love very much.

Perhaps I would not have had this central feeling of ease had I not known that I could depart whenever I liked. True, I had to earn my living, but I had earned it elsewhere before then, and could earn it elsewhere again. I was in this queer, melancholy town of my own choice, and for a limited time. I was not under life-sentence to the Vizcayan rain. It was easy to be absent-mindedly content.

I remember that I began with earnestness on the Spanish language. I bought dictionaries and grammars, and classic works of literature. Sacramentals of Calderón and a volume or two of Lope de Vega; and Pepita Jimenez, with which I never made headway. Unamuno and Ruben Dario, and, because he won the Nobel Prize that year, Benavente, whom I translated to myself with pleasure. I remember that when I told a certain cultured elderly Spaniard I was reading Benavente, he looked grave; said no young woman should read him, and recommended

Hermana San Sulpicio, which is the novel every Spaniard recommended in those days to every foreign young lady.

I bought *Don Quixote*, too, and though it was long before I could read it with real pleasure—I have said that then, as now, I was lazy—already when I was only struggling wearily with it, it gave me delight, and considerable enlightenment in approach to it, to listen to Spaniards talk together of that book. They really know it, really like to talk of it, and quote it, and chuckle, and cap each other's quotations. Certain unpretentious conversations which I half followed that winter taught me much about *Don Quixote*.

But I did not really learn Spanish. I learnt rather quickly to talk and understand on the surface, to skim the newspapers and guess the content and emotion of an easy poem. I forsook my grammars then, and have never really learnt Spanish. At night in my room overlooking the harbour I read Castilian sometimes and looked up words as I went —but more often I read English, or wrote English. Letters, and those dreadful whimsical articles, and part of a short story, and the first act of what would have been an extremely sentimental comedy.

I remember the ships swinging up and down the Nervión—I watched them from my window. Ships of all the world, and among them the *Mar Canta-brico*, now at the bottom of the sea with its cargo of help for the Republic.

I remember the commuters' electric train between the town and Portugalete on the north-west corner of the river mouth. It ran by the river and through the premises of the most famous foundries —the 'Vizcaya,' the 'Altos Hornos,' the 'Santa Ana'—where the great fires never went out and where half-naked men moved like unreal creatures through glare and darkness. I remember the slum suburbs about those furnaces—El Desierto, Sestao —savage and shameless in poverty, but very gay on Sundays, with *harmonicas* playing up and down the stations and young men and women, shining and neat, crowding on to the train to go and dance at a *verbena* in Santurce. I remember the talk in those crowded trains, and how I strained to understand it—though everyone wanted to practise his English on me and everyone seemed to know a few English words. All classes in Bilbao were very Anglophil. But I liked it better when they talked among themselves and took no notice of me.

The average Bilbaino is ribald and tough in humour. Not as urbane and dry as the joker-of Madrid, but with an appreciation none the less of malice. He likes to give and receive strong comment and enjoys exaggeration so long as it is not in the direction of whimsicality, which I do not think he would understand at all. I was often reminded of Irish talk, particularly of the talk of my native Munster, as I listened in these trains in Bilbao. (Madrid's conversation is reminiscent of Dublin's.) At lunch yesterday someone spoke of the Irish predilection for "the fun of the phrase," and if 'fun' be understood as a kind of horseplay, then that describes something which Munster and Vizcaya seem to enjoy in common. The explosive, strong fun of the phrase. They are very good at ribaldry in Bilbao, and so are we in Munster. But I think that they are perhaps the more kind-hearted people.

I remember Portugalete—old, wild village and neat suburban retreat—with the river running fast beside it and at the corner of the *muelle* becoming the bay. The Sunday morning market in the arcaded *plaza*, pimientos and pomegranates, hand-kerchiefs and rope-soled shoes, roses, flat maize-loaves, butter wrapped in green ferns. The crazy, uphill streets, the noble late Gothic church upon the hill, the neat parade beside the water with the *guardia civil* irritably preventing children from falling over the parapet, and bourgeois ladies in black sitting in perpetual idleness and watchfulness

behind their shining *miradores*. The little carrier-
bridge which, like a suspended lift, runs to and fro
between the *muelle* and Las Arenas, and will give
you a ride for a halfpenny. Las Arenas, Bilbao's
pleasure settlement, beach, yacht club, 'Dancing,'
and ostentatious villas. A lifeless, boring place, like
new Algorta beyond it. But old Algorta too, a
fishing village, crooked and cracked as Clovelly but
mercifully unaware of its fatal picturesqueness.
The coast further on. I remember walks in the
wind above a leonine sea. How green the cliff-tops
were—like Ireland—and how changeful and thrill-
ing the sky. I remember a white lighthouse, and
windflowers and wild orchids in the grass. And
chacoli drunk in the loneliest village café I have
ever found.

I remember the shops in the two long, lively
shopping streets of old Bilbao. The jewellery, the
turrón, the astounding corsets and *brassières*. I
remember the comforting teashop where English
and Irish exiles huddled and grumbled on wet
afternoons. The dove-cote on the Arenal—a funny
affair—and the vast Town Hall of which Bilbao is
so proud. Very ugly indeed. I remember sitting
often by San Vicente which I liked to look at and
found very lovely. I liked to watch the dancing
too at night in the squares, under the harsh lights,

among the clipped plane-trees. Very beautiful and deliberate modern dancing.

I remember flowers everywhere, in all weathers, perpetual leafage, camellia bushes laden. Bright flower-pots in military lines, strawberries red under their leaves in December. Mud, and everyone soaking. Starved, sore-headed children in swarms, unemployed men leaning over the *puente*. Marvellous limousines. Delicious food. Always the flaring furnaces, the moving boats, the strong lights of trolley tracks down the hills. Brassy music on the Arenal, crowds in the Café del Boulevard. Yellow trams lurching. Good Friday processions and the smell of ten thousand wax candles. Bull-fights, *verbenas*, manifestos, strikes. Brilliant weather, dreadful weather. Newspaper jokes on Holy Innocents' Day. The evening *paseito*. Fishermen singing *flamenco* by the water-steps. And everywhere—about Morocco, about Basque Nationalism, about agrarian and foundry troubles, about all Bilbao's thousand woes—writing on the wall. Always plenty of writing on the wall. But no one seemed to read it.

It will be seen that sitting up here near Our Lady of Begoña I have remembered nothing much, nothing of great general or personal interest from that lost year. But I see now

THE CHURCH OF SAN VICENTE, BILBAO

that, though smudgy, it was a more indelible year
for me than many. I am glad to have had it, and
glad to sit here again with its unimpressive
memories.

ARRIBA, ESPAÑA!

SO good-bye, *turismo*. Here is Irun. Here is
the Bidasoa bridge which we first crossed so
many years ago in August rains and now must
cross in August rain again—but going the wrong
way. Here is the solid man in black, his overcoat
caped—imperturbably reflecting.

There is no more to be said. There is nothing
left for our sentimental tourists to do but go home
and put their suitcases in the attic. And wait for
war—nothing better than that—to strike a country
so deserving of more helpful things, so much in
need of them. And wait for the outcome of that
war before beginning to dream of future harmless
sentimental wanderings, not merely in Spain but
anywhere. Wait to see if there will be anywhere
safe to wander in, or even if they will be allowed
to live to get down their suitcases. For though it
has always been Spain's way to play a lone hand—
even she can be allowed to do that no longer, and
in any case, say only Spaniards were fighting this

218

war it is being fought for an issue which is everyone's immediate concern everywhere. It is a war
waged by the forces of militaristic absolutism
against democracy. However anti-Communist you
may be and however you may deplore the burning
of churches or the penalising of the traditional
religion of Spain, you cannot, if you take the
trouble to read the 1931 Constitution, deny its
dignity, justice, humanity, efficiency and natural
idealism. Nor can you claim that therein the
Church is more than disestablished and politically
controlled. And it is a fact that though certain
details of these measures of control were much
disputed they were in the main accepted by an
actively Catholic nation as reasonable and sound.
This Constitution was established at great cost and
after an admirably bloodless revolution. In the five
years from its establishment to the outbreak of war,
Spain, hopeful and active at first and in many ways
visibly and usefully busy with reform, had then
fallen into a reaction of disappointment and something like despair on the one hand, and backsliding
and cowardice on the other. But the Republic
stood, and offered legitimate means for statesmanship to force Spain forward to the decent social
state set out in its legally established Constitution.
When the Radicals Samper and Lerroux held

office in 1934, and when Gil Robles was making wild boasts all over the place to his popular Action following—in that year Asturias and Catalonia lost patience, and struck hard at the relaxed and inactive government. But because it was not being what it had set out to be—not because they wanted its Constitution overthrown. Said Companys on October 5th, 1934—"Recent events have given all citizens the clear impression that the Republic, as to its fundamental democratic principles, is in the gravest peril."

And he was only too right. We all know the dreary story of autumn 1934 in Spain and all the woes that followed from it, and it is no doubt true that by now, had Fascism not decided to overthrow the Spanish Constitution, Communism would have started a war of aggression to remake it. A war which all my Communist friends in this country would hold as holy as they hold Franco's outbreak to be criminal. But I would deplore the Communistic aggression—being that funny old-fashioned thing, a pacifist. I hold no war-maker holy, and I cannot foresee that I ever will. But at least a war waged on the clear insistence—that government of the people by the people for the people shall not perish from the earth is one very impressive if horrible way of saying something which must never, never be denied—whereas a war such as General Franco's, openly aimed at the murder of every democratic principle, and for the setting up of his little self as yet another Mussolini —such a war strikes not merely for the death of Spain, but at every decent dream or effort for humanity everywhere. It kills not only the slow, creeping growths, the sensitive plants of social and economic justice which the last hundred years have gardened so painfully and at so great a price, but it sterilises the whole future. Makes it practically impossible to begin again. In short, if the Mussolini-Hitler idea is to win in Europe, then it is good-bye to all humanity's small, patient, but once living hopes of universalised decency of life. Why? Because, whatever sentimental sops the interviewed Fascist leaders may throw out as to their benevolent, personal notions for making us all happy—their root inspiration is both idiotic and pernicious. It is the glorification of one silly nationalism above another. It is conceit and jingoism, and "look at me!" It is the assertion of one bully's ego, and his claim to patronise and allocate the destinies of millions of his fellows, without the faintest reference to *their* egos and *their* claims. Whereas—loathe manifest Communism as you please, point to Stalin and say: "What is he but a

rampant Fascist bully?—dread even as I do the
Communistic insult to individualism and spiritual
freedom—it is yet true that, at its most dubious
and depressing, the root inspiration of Communism is simply the old, old generosity and
decency of a few of the world's saints. "From each
according to his ability to each according to his
need." That is the corner-stone of Communism,
however misguidedly practising Communists may
seem to build on it. It was also Saint Teresa's
eternal cry, and is to be found, almost word for
word, in several of her writings. And for this
reason it is probable—*pace The Universe* and the
Catholic Herald—that she, indomitable fighter,
would have been to-day on the side of Valencia and
Madrid. For though she could split hairs with any
intellectual, and see the hundred sides of every
human issue, in action or for getting things done
she believed in setting one broad principle against
the other, choosing the truer and chancing the
minor consequences. So long as the spring-idea
was noble, Teresa, knowing humanity, did not fuss
overmuch about incidental difficulties and differences. All that she asked was that fantastic thing—
idealism. "Accustom yourselves to have great
desires." Given the generous impulse, she could
manage the incidental traps and foibles. What she

would not have or listen to was pomp and circum-
stance. She gave cheek in and out of season to the
Papal Nuncio in Spain, and liked nothing better
than to have a crow over spoilt and luxurious pre-
lates. She was all for the setting down, simplifica-
tion and reduction to their true duties and true
humility of the religious orders. To get them poor
and simple and ship-shape was her life-work, and
I do not think that her shrewd brain would see
anything profoundly dangerous to them in the
legislation for their control of the Constitution of
the Second Republic. And to tell the truth, I find
it impossible to imagine that in this present war so
generous a soldier would be pacifist. Which I
regret to have to admit, holding all war to be
barbarous and ignoble. But at least the attacked,
the non-aggressor may be sympathised with when
an adventurer, unasked, marches a lot of foreigners
into his house to set it in order for him. *"Cet
animal est très méchant; quand on l'attaque il se
défend."* The Spanish Republic was attacked, and by
those forces of reaction and petty nationalism which
can never justify themselves in the eyes of the sane.
So in this case, watching Spain's agony, seeing it as
a key struggle for the democratic principle, one's
pacificism is indeed pressed hard by natural rage
and sympathy.

And if the ultimate, difficult victory is with Madrid and the Republic—what then? Will Spain become a rigid, collectivist union of soviets? Improbable in the end. In this so long overdue convulsion and upheaval of ideas it may take a very complicated people a considerable time to work out to the true beginnings of a new and reasonable destiny. Spain at the 'Cease Fire,' if it ever comes, will have a very difficult garden to cultivate. But the will and the brains are there, as well as vast, mismanaged material for prosperity. The people are natural aristocrats, which means that they are profoundly democratic. But they are also astoundingly individualistic and inclined to meditation and mysticism. They can be controlled by a broad ideal and by a symbol which appeals to them, but within that ideal the rules must be limber and have all possible room for personality—which is why, taking it broad and large, the Catholic faith has remained so native to the Spaniard. It seems unlikely that the regimentation of Russian Communism could work at all in Spain. Given half a chance, with time and luck the Peninsula will perhaps resolve itself into a loosely-linked federation of small, democratic states, all governed for external purposes from a centre, but internally run on regional, distributive principles. Always assuming, of course—a large assumption—that our modern blustering Cæsars can be told in plain language where they get off. Which does not seem possible.

Still, let us be silly and hope while we yet live. Let us dream that the end of everything decent and lovable is not yet. Let us even imagine that Spain, having gone through her hell before our eyes, may actually succeed in giving our nitwitted world the fright and the pause it needs so pointedly, and that, having done us the service of being our cockpit, she may be allowed to heal, crawl back to life and even provide our children's children with some sort of working model of how justice and individualism may flourish together.

Because in the Spanish character they can and do. Everyone who knows Spain knows how impressively the man in the street, the reflective middle-aged man in black, can be scrupulous, kindly and understanding towards his neighbour and yet in himself a rock of pride and non-committal gravity. It is their secret to be highly vitalised and yet detached from life. Warm and cold, generous and secretive. Out of such a nature it *should* be possible to build a reasonable way of life, a gentlemanly, anarchical system founded on man's supposed predisposition to sanity.

But this is the twentieth century and no one believes any longer—not even the slow, reflective Spaniard—that we are sane.

As I write the Spanish battle wages desperately again round Guadalajara, for possession of the Madrid–Valencia road. Terrible as it is, it must seem a small military exercise to all the world powers massing their tanks and airplane carriers for the next really big all-in affair. And someone has said in *The Times* that if the Republican Army can keep that road open for ever, Madrid can hold out for ever. So it becomes not merely of practical but of symbolical importance—the Madrid–Valencia road. If it is kept open, then some of the ideas and hopes that make life tolerable will survive —to fight another day. Which—we must try to have the courage to say—is something. But God, for peace! For statesmanship instead of poison gas, for sanity instead of megalomania, for faith in man instead of theoretical fanaticism!

Well, good-bye, Spain. All that we can do, the lazy and helpless, is lull ourselves with remembering. Had we the power truly to set down our memories, how nobly you should be praised. But words are threadbare as your scene never is. I shall remember always a million things not set down in this book or anywhere—moments and places

226

without name or date, but filled with your light and arched for ever by your incomparable sky. Fatal attraction between persons is an old poets' notion that some of us still like to believe is possible and occasional, though not probable—and Spain seems to me to be the *femme fatale* among countries. Though many would claim that for lovely France. For me, however, it has been Spain. So true is this that I have hardly seen any other countries. Always I go back over the Pyrenees. My love has been long and slow—lazy and selfish too, but I know that wherever I go henceforward and whatever I see I shall never again be able to love an earthly scene as I have loved the Spanish. Except some bits of Ireland, bits of home. But that is different. Though Ireland is as beautiful as any country on earth, I am native to her, and therefore cannot feel the novel thrill of her attraction. One does not mix up the love one feels for a parent with the infatuations of adult life. And with Spain I am once and for all infatuated. With curious fidelity—for I am fickle.

So I remember and mourn as the new ruins fall into place. Spain had her share of ruins. But Madrid was poor in them, poor in ancientry, though capital of Castile. Rich in sun, children and acacia-trees, and in fine, new and vulgar

buildings. Rich in her sense of the fun and rightness of life; rich in friendliness, bull-fights and
good pictures. Ah, again to see Lalanda take his
bull, once, twice and almost three times across the
Ventas ring on his own invented *mariposa*. *Mariposa*
means 'butterfly', and Lalanda, holding his cape
behind him as if it were wings, would draw the bull
where he pleased, the horn almost resting on his
silk, with flicks of the right wing and then of the
left. Of grace and bravery and the control of each
by the other there can be nothing more exemplary
under the sun. And how the sun shone on those
corridas—except sometimes in September when
for the fifth and sixth bull the great white arc-lights
went on, and one saw the ancient art newly illu-
mined. That was very interesting—the effect of
cold lighting and pallor on all the brave glitter.
And afterwards it was dark when we left the ring
and walked slowly, slowly through the seething
crowds all the way down to Alcalá under the
shining trees and sat there drinking and watching
with a contentment that seemed as if it could never
tire the gay Sunday night life of the gay, gracious
people. Though the imperturbable *madrileños* still
sit in their cafés, I believe, and even in one of
them keep Franco's table reserved and ready for
him—*pour rire*, because he was rash enough to

boast last December that he would drink coffee in the Puerta in January—though they still sit and drink and laugh at Franco, there are ruins about them, and losses and burials in their secretive hearts. And there is always this question to the east of the Madrid–Valencia road. May it be held open for ever and for all our sakes! Meantime good-bye, and *Arriba, España!*

THE END

London.   *October 1936–February 1937.*